A JOURNEY OF RICHES

Abundant Living

12 Insights for Living a Plentiful Life

Published by Motion Media International
Editors: Vanessa Correia, Ishka Gupta, and Daniel Decillis
Cover Design: Motion Media International
Typesetting & Assembly: Motion Media International
Printing: Amazon and Ingram Sparks

Creator: John Spender - Primary Author
Title: *A Journey Of Riches – Abundant Living*
ISBN Digital: 978-1-925919-32-5
ISBN Print: 978-1-925919-33-2
Categories: Self-Help, Business & Economics & Personal Success and Spirituality

Acknowledgments

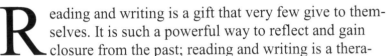

R eading and writing is a gift that very few give to themselves. It is such a powerful way to reflect and gain closure from the past; reading and writing is a therapeutic process. The experience raises one's self-esteem, confidence and awareness of self.

I learned this when I collated the first book in the *A Journey of Riches* series, which now includes twenty-five books with over 260 different co-authors from more than forty different countries. It's not easy to write about your personal experiences, and I honor and respect every one of the authors who have collaborated in the series thus far.

For many of the authors, English is their second language, which is a significant achievement in itself. In creating this anthology of short stories, I have been touched by the amount of generosity, gratitude and shared energy that this experience has given everyone.

The inspiration for *A Journey of Riches, Abundant Living* came from my experiences of living in Bali particular this last year in Amed. I would often notice many different forms of abundance from fields of banana's, papaya trees, the rolling hills and of course the amazing ocean views all made me feel abundant. *Of course*, I could not have created this book without the eleven other co-authors who all said YES when I asked them to share their insights and wisdom. Just as each chapter in this book makes for inspiring reading, each story represents one chapter in the life of each of the authors, with the chief aim of having you, the reader, live a more inspired life. Together, we can overcome our fears and live a more fulfilling abundant adventure.

I want to thank all the authors for entrusting me with their unique memories, encounters and wisdom. Thank you for sharing and opening the door to your soul so that others may learn from your experience. I trust the readers will gain confidence from your successes, and also wisdom from your failures.

I also want to thank my family. I know you are proud of me, seeing how far I have come from that ten-year-old boy who was learning how to read and write at a basic level. Big shout out to my Mom, Robert, Dad, Merril; my brother Adam and his daughter Krystal; my sister Hollie, her partner Brian, my nephew Charlie and niece, Heidi; thank you for your support. Also, kudos to my grandparents, Gran and Pop, who are alive and well, and Ma and Pa, who now rest in peace. They accept me just the way I am with all my travels and adventures around the world.

Thanks to all the team at Motion Media International; you have done an excellent job at editing and collating this book. It was a pleasure working with you on this successful project, and I thank you for your patience in dealing with the various changes and adjustments along the way.

Thank you, the reader, for having the courage to look at your life and how you can improve your future in a fast and rapidly changing world.

Thank you again to my fellow co-authors: Belinda Foster, Samuel Sykes II, Harmony Polo, Anastasia Gunawan, Abhinav Gupta, Lanelle Martin, Sam Frazer, Catherine Kavadas, Lili Galera, Travis Gray, AJ Myers,

We would greatly appreciate an honest review on Amazon if this book inspires you. This is how we gain more readers to find our inspiring book!

With gratitude,
John Spender

Praise For A Journey of Riches Book Series

"The A Journey of Riches book series is a great collection of inspiring short stories that will leave you wanting more!"

~ Alex Hoffmann, Network Marketing Guru.

"If you are looking for an inspiring read to get you through any change, this is it!! This book is comprised of many gripping perspectives from a collection of successful international authors with a tone of wisdom to share."

~ Theera Phetmalaigul, Entrepreneur/Investor.

"A Journey of Riches is an empowering series that implements two simple words in overcoming life's struggles.

By diving into the meaning of the words "problem" and "challenge," you will find yourself motivated to believe in the triumph of perseverance. With many different authors from all around the world coming together to share various stories of life's trials, you will find yourself drenched in encouragement to push through even the darkest of battles.

The stories are heartfelt personal shares of moving through and transforming challenges into rich life experiences.

The book will move, touch and inspire your spirit to face and overcome any of life's adversities. It is a truly inspirational read. Thank you for being the kind, open soul you are, John!!"

~ Casey Plouffe, Seven Figure Network Marketer.

"A must-read for anyone facing major changes or challenges in life right now. This book will give you the courage to move through any struggle with confidence, grace and ease."

~ Jo-Anne Irwin, Transformational Coach and Best Selling Author.

"I have enjoyed the *A Journey of Riches* book series. Each person's story is written from the heart, and everyone's journey is different. We all have a story to tell, and John Spender does an amazing job of finding authors and combining their stories into uplifting books."

~ Liz Misner Palmer, Foreign Service Officer.

"A timely read as I'm facing a few challenges right now. I like the various insights from the different authors. This book will inspire you to move through any challenge or change that you are experiencing."

~ David Ostrand, Business Owner.

"I've known John Spender for a while now, and I was blessed with an opportunity to be in book four in the series. I know that you will enjoy this new journey, like the rest of the books in the series. The collection of stories will assist you with making changes, dealing with challenges and seeing that transformation is possible for your life."

~ Charlie O' Shea, Entrepreneur.

"*A Journey of Riches* series will draw you in and help you dig deep into your soul. These authors have unbelievable life stories of purpose inside of them. John Spender is dedicated to bringing peace, love and adventure to the world of his readers! Dive into this series, and you will be transformed!"

~ Jeana Matichak, Author of *Finding Peace*.

"Awesome! Truly inspirational! It is amazing what the human spirit can achieve and overcome! Highly recommended!!"

~ Fabrice Beliard, Australian Business Coach and Best Selling Author.

"*A Journey of Riches* series is a must-read. It is an empowering collection of inspirational and moving stories, full of courage, strength and heart. Bringing peace and awareness to those lucky enough to read to assist and inspire them on their life journey."

~ Gemma Castiglia, Avalon Healing, Best Selling Author.

"The *A Journey of Riches* book series is an inspirational collection of books that will empower you to take on any challenge or change in life."

~ Kay Newton, Midlife Stress Buster, and Best Selling Author.

"*A Journey of Riches* book series is an inspiring collection of stories, sharing many different ideas and perspectives on how to overcome challenges, deal with change and to make empowering choices in your life. Open the book anywhere and let your mood choose where you need to read. Buy one of the books today; you'll be glad that you did!"

~ Trish Rock, Modern Day Intuitive, Best Selling Author, Speaker, Psychic & Holistic Coach.

"*A Journey of Riches* is another inspiring read. The authors are from all over the world, and each has a unique perspective to share that will have you thinking differently about your current circumstances in life. An insightful read!"

~ Alexandria Calamel, Success Coach and Best Selling Author.

"The *A Journey of Riches* book series is a collection of real-life stories, which are truly inspiring and give you the confidence that no matter what you are dealing with in your life, there is a light at the end of the tunnel, and a very bright one at that. Totally empowering!"

~ John Abbott, Freedom Entrepreneur.

"An amazing collection of true stories from individuals who have overcome great changes, and who have transformed their lives and used their experience to uplift, inspire and support others."

~ Carol Williams, Author, Speaker & Coach.

"You can empower yourself from the power within this book that can help awaken the sleeping giant within you. John has a purpose in life to bring inspiring people together to share their wisdom for the benefit of all who venture deep into this book series. If you are looking for inspiration to be someone special, this book can be your guide."

~ Bill Bilwani, Renowned Melbourne Restaurateur.

"In the *A Journey of Riches* series, you will catch the impulse to step up, reconsider and settle for only the very best for yourself and those around you. Penned from the heart and with an unflinching drive to make a difference for the good of all, *A Journey of Riches* series is a must-read."

~ Steve Coleman, author of *Decisions, Decisions! How to Make the Right One Every Time.*

"Do you want to be on top of your game? *A Journey of Riches* is a must-read with breakthrough insights that will help you do just that!"

~ Christopher Chen, Entrepreneur.

"In *A Journey of Riches*, you will find the insight, resources and tools you need to transform your life. By reading the author's stories, you, too, can be inspired to achieve your greatest accomplishments and what is truly possible for you. Reading this book activates your true potential for transforming your life way beyond what you think is possible. Read it and learn how you, too, can have a magical life."

~ Elaine Mc Guinness, Best Selling Author of *Unleash Your Authentic Self!*

"If you are looking for an inspiring read, look no further than the A Journey of Riches book series. The books are an inspiring collection of short stories that will encourage you to embrace life even more. I highly recommend you read one of the books today!"

~ Kara Dono, Doula, Healer and Best Selling Author.

"*A Journey of Riches* series is a must-read for anyone seeking to enrich their own lives and gain wisdom through the wonderful stories of personal empowerment & triumphs over life's challenges. I've given several copies to my family, friends and clients to inspire and support them to step into their greatness.

I highly recommend that you read these books, savoring the many 'aha's' and tools you will discover inside."

~ Michele Cempaka, Hypnotherapist, Shaman, Transformational Coach & Reiki Master.

"If you are looking for an inspirational read, look no further than the *A Journey of Riches* book series. The books are an inspiring and educational collection of short stories from the author's soul that will encourage you to embrace life even more. I've even given them to my clients, too, so that their journeys inspire them in life for wealth, health and everything else in between. I recommend you make it a priority to read one of the books today!"

~ Goro Gupta, Chief Education Officer, Mortgage Terminator, Property Mentor.

"The A Journey of Riches book series is filled with real-life short stories of heartfelt tribulations turned into uplifting, self-transformation by the power of the human spirit to overcome adversity. The journeys captured in these books will encourage you to embrace life in a whole new way. I highly recommend reading this inspiring anthology series."

~ Chris Drabenstott, Best Selling Author, and Editor.

"There is so much motivational power in the A Journey of Riches series!! Each book is a compilation of inspiring, real-life stories by several different authors, which makes the journey feel more relatable and success more attainable. If you are looking for something to move you forward, you'll find it in one (or all) of these books."

~ Cary MacArthur, Personal Empowerment Coach

"I've been fortunate to write with John Spender and now, I call him a friend. A Journey of Riches book series features real stories that have inspired me and will inspire you. John has a passion for finding amazing people from all over the world, giving the series a global perspective on relevant subject matters."

~ Mike Campbell, Fat Guy Diary, LLC

"The *A Journey of Riches* series is the reflection of beautiful souls who have discovered the fire within. Each story takes you inside the truth of what truly matters in life. While reading these stories, my heart space expanded to understand that our most significant contribution in this lifetime is to give and receive love. May you also feel inspired as you read this book."

~ Katie Neubaum, Author of *Transformation Calling*.

"*A Journey of Riches* is an inspiring testament that love and gratitude are the secret ingredients to living a happy and fulfilling life. This series is sure to inspire and bless your life in a big way. Truly an inspirational read that is written and created by real people, sharing real-life stories about the power and courage of the human spirit."

~ Jen Valadez, Emotional Intuitive and Best Selling Author

Table of Contents

Preface

I collated this book and chose the various authors to share their experiences about how they live an abundant life. The eclectic collection of chapters encompass a myriad of different writing styles and perspectives that demonstrate what is possible when we take action and connect into the unlimited supply of abundance.

Like all of us, each author has a unique story and insight to share with you. It might so happen that one or more authors have lived through an experience similar to circumstances in your life. Their words could be just the words you need to read to help you through your challenges and motivate you to continue on your chosen path.

Storytelling has been the way humankind has communicated ideas and learning throughout our civilization. While we have become more sophisticated with technology and living in the modern world is more convenient, there is still much discontent and dissatisfaction. Many people have also moved away from reading books, and they are missing valuable information that can help them move forward in life with a positive outlook. Moving towards the tasks or dreams that scare us breeds confidence growing towards becoming better versions of ourselves.

I think it is essential to turn off the T.V.; to slow down and to read, reflect, and take the time to appreciate everything you have in life. Start with an anthology book as they offer a cornucopia of viewpoints relating to a particular theme. In this case, it's abundance and how others live abundantly. I think the reason we feel stuck in life or have challenges in a particular area is because we see the problem through the same lens that created it. With this compendium and all of the books in the *A Journey of Riches* series, you have many different writing styles and perspectives that will help you think and see your challenges differently, motivating you to elevate your set of circumstances.

Anthology books are also great because you can start from any chapter and gain valuable insight or a nugget of wisdom without the feeling that you have missed something from the earlier episodes.

I love reading many different types of personal development books because learning and personal growth are vital. If you are not learning and growing, well, you're staying the same. Everything in the universe is growing, expanding, and changing. If we are not open to different ideas and a multitude of ways to think and be, then even the most skilled and educated among us can become close-minded.

The concept of this book series is to open you up to diverse ways of perceiving your reality. It is to encourage you and give you many avenues of thinking about the same subject. My wish for you is to feel empowered to make a decision that will best suit you in moving forward with your life. As Albert Einstein said, **"We cannot solve problems with the same level of thinking that created them."** With Einstein's words in mind, let your mood pick a chapter in the book, or read from the beginning to the end and be guided to find the answers you seek.

 If you feel inspired, we would love an honest review on Amazon. This will help create awareness around this fantastic series of books.

With gratitude,
John Spender

**"THE WHOLE SECRET OF
ABUNDANCE LIVING CAN BE
SUMMED UP ON THIS
SENTENCE:
'NOT YOUR RESPONSIBILITY
BUT YOUR RESPONSE TO GOD'S
ABILITY'."**

~ Carl F H Henry

CHAPTER ONE

The Seachronicity Of Abundant Living

By Belinda Foster

I was headed to my car on a chilly January morning in 2021 when I heard my sweet neighbor Anna open her sliding glass door to say, "Good morning!"

"Good Morning!" I responded. "I'm so sorry I haven't stopped by to have coffee with you. Been a bit busy with work, plus I'm writing a chapter for a book and, well, uh…I'm sorta stuck! Got any tips, since you're a published author?" "What's the subject?" she excitedly asked. "Abundant living, my journey to abundance?" Seems I wasn't sure if I was telling her or asking her!

I further explained, "My thoughts keep darting off in a million directions. I don't even know where to start!"

"Here's what I want you to do today," Anna quickly responded. "Think of three words or phrases that come to mind when you think of abundance. Write them down. That's all. Start there and then watch the journey unfold," she said with a big ole smile.

"Wow. That's good advice, Anna. Thank you. I will."

And that's how Anna's smile got on my list of three things that day, because she was right. And from her suggestion, her smile and to my keyboard, my journey of *Abundant Living* story began.

Memories started gushing like a geyser.

Looking back over the years, I guess I had my fair share of tough times but somehow managed to plow through them. Don't we all know what it feels like to go through financial hardship, breakups, conflict, and loss? For the longest time, I thought my life wasn't the way I wanted it to be, or these negative events wouldn't be happening. I had been conditioned to think that lack and suffering were just part of life.

But mixed in there were also my happiest moments, like a proposal, the birth of my sister's and friend's children, good times exploring, experiencing that first deep love, recognizing the blessing of a healthy family, having friends to hug, and those crazy people who keep it fun and a lot less boring along the way.

Take a minute now and reflect on your happiest moments. Think about a few good people who have crossed your path, the good times where you've laughed the hardest, and those good feelings that still make you smile to this day. These positive feelings are the strongest combination of ingredients that create your magnetic elixir for an abundant life.

Magnets attract. Your happy elixir of feelings is your internal universe saying yes, I'll have more of that. Good jobs, great family, amazing friends, excellent health, steady financial flow, and, best of all, the strangers who show up randomly on your path. Or are they randomly appearing?

No, they're not random for me and they aren't for you, either. I have also repeatedly prayed that the right people at the right time would cross my path. They came, and they continue to come.

Take, for example, the man in the airport bookstore who— without even turning around to see who was behind him—

passed a book over his shoulder and said, "This one." It just happened to be exactly what I was seeking at the time, a better understanding of God. How did he know this? Yes, I was in the self-help section, but there were hundreds of titles, subjects, and paths to personal and spiritual development. And yet, he and I had had no conversation.

The book was *God's Breath*. It was a seeker's book about God and how God is defined in sacred texts from seven teachings around the world. I needed to understand all sacred beliefs about the universe, the cosmos, this earth, other planets, the moon, the sun, and the stars before I could understand anything. I had an unstoppable desire not only to seek but to connect to what made sense.

I describe my earlier years as if I'm watching a movie with someone else playing the role of a younger me. My first attempts at adulting kicked me in the rear. Doesn't every 18-year-old wake up in their first run down rental house to no heat because they let the natural gas tank and firewood run out? No problem! I packed up my office attire, make-up, shampoo, soap, towel, and hair dryer, and made it to the bank at 6:30am before anyone else arrived so I could at least be warm while I prepared for work, at work. Oh, the crazy adventures I've had!

It was another book suggestion by a friend in 1993 that once again changed the way I viewed abundance. *The Power is Within You* by Louise Hay gave me an abundant mindset shift when I was in between banking jobs starting my own health coaching business. The first few months were tough. I had doubts about making it. I'd come home to a mailbox of nothing but bills for just basic needs like utilities and rent for a low-end apartment and was barely breaking even.

From the wisdom of Louise Hay, I learned that my mindset is what needed to change, so that bills no longer scared me like they once did. She advised that I be thankful for each bill because it meant I had already been provided the service and I was trusted to pay later. What a beautiful way to think about bills! And sure enough, that shift started to parallel the growth in my clientele, and the anxiety about bills was no longer a problem.

She had me envision myself standing in front of an ocean, with permission to take all the water that I wanted. What vessel was I using? Was I standing there with a thimble? A bucket? I was so proud that I was standing there with a barrel…until she said a pipeline! Wow. It became clear I had been way too limiting in my thoughts and beliefs!

A few decades have passed and a few more wrinkles have appeared since I've come to understand that it is in the mind that our thoughts express a feeling, good or bad. And it is also in the mind that a feeling inspires a thought, good or bad.

It is through this mental and emotional tug of war between our thoughts and the heart's feelings that our universe takes shape. In other words, if instead of focusing on the negative feelings I focused on the positive, then the things I don't want to happen won't happen. And the things I do want to happen, will.

Test it out for yourself. Think of something you would so love to have or experience. What are the good feelings being aroused as you consider having that thing or experience? Hold onto these feelings because they are energetically pulling the pieces together to craft your universe of abundance, right now.

I'd be remiss not to mention money when speaking about abundant living. I'd also like to say abundance isn't about money. But I can't. Because the truth is, money is something we've all agreed on as having value. Money represents currency, as in your energy current. If we have negative feelings about currency, chances are we won't have much money. If we have positive feelings about currency, we will most likely have more money. We all use it, so why not think good about it, with it, and in using it. Or, better yet, why don't we imagine a world where everything is free? Wouldn't that be a fun experience!

Year after year, twists and turns in this journey of life continue to give me an abundance of experiences that I would have never thought possible. I can honestly say I now better understand the true meaning of abundance. Abundance is in everything, and it comes at the most perfect time and in the most magical ways.

I recall fondly in 1992 when I had the pleasure of spending time with Loring Sagan and his family, through the connection of a mutual friend. Loring is the son of Ginetta Sagan, who was imprisoned, raped, and tortured by Italian fascists during World War II but survived to help build Amnesty International. Loring's father was Dr. Leonard Sagan, a distinguished physician, humanitarian, and renowned researcher on human longevity and the impact of radiating electromagnetic fields of the power grid.

At that time, I had no idea who Ginetta Sagan was or the impact of her humanitarian works on advancing global human rights. I had no idea in the early 90s that radiating frequencies from towers were harmful. Yet, ironically, in 2016, I became involved in working with the electromagnetic biotech health industry. I would never have guessed back in the early 90s that Leonard Sagan's work would be even remotely close to mine, nor would I have guessed that in 2021, as I write this, that people globally are coming together with one heart like never before to stop the abuse of power, people, and children by abusive government regimes.

The most compelling philosophical discussion I ever had with Loring and his father was how the 'the Universe always says yes.' "What did that mean?" I asked.

"It means that whatever you believe, good or bad, the Universe says yes. If you believe life is hard and you'll always be poor, the Universe will agree with you and make that happen. If you believe life is easy, and that all things are abundantly available to you, including money, then the Universe says yes and will make that happen." they explained.

It took me many years to understand what they were saying. I came to realize the Universe is about spiritual laws, and just like the law of gravity, where it pays to understand that jumping off a 20-story building isn't a good idea, it pays to understand the spiritual laws as well. Our spiritual laws seek harmony, and you get to decide what harmony means for you. The harmony is found in your thoughts and feelings, when the two come together as one.

It was in 2014, at the age of 54, that I was introduced to another phrase I have come to love: 'act as if.' Act? 'As if' what? You mean act as if I already have what I'm looking for, whether that's more experiences, a new car, money, or more friends? Whether that's a healthier lifestyle, better eyesight, or a perfect soulmate? How do you 'act' like you have something you do not? The idea of 'acting as if' that thing or desire had already happened didn't initially feel right to me. It felt incongruent. Was it being honest with myself to 'act'?

I had read the teachings of great wisdom masters Earl Nightingale and Dr. Wayne Dyer, along with more recent works like those of Dr. Joe Dispenza, Dr. Greg Bradden, and some lesser-known favorites, too. The works of Wallace Wattles and *Feeling is the Secret* by Neville Goddard, as well as *Working with the Law*, by Raymond Holliwell, are among my favorites. I realized that just like in *God's Breath*, they all said the same thing in different ways. 'Act as if' was really no different than 'the universe says yes.'

Why would we ever 'act as if' if the 'if' is something negative we don't want? Good or bad, the universe will say, "Yes, let me help you with that." Powerful!

Opening my mind to these spiritual laws always takes me back to my youth and growing up in the church where my seeking began. The sermons and Sunday school lessons talked a lot about faith without works and works without faith. I can't really say I understood any of this as a child, much less as an adult.

We were taught to work hard, be a good person, and to pray. I have done a ton of praying in my lifetime, let me tell you! Yet, it was clear that either my prayers weren't being heard or that it wasn't in God's will. Perhaps it was both. Now what? Have more faith and work harder. That's all I had known.

If free will is God's will, then wouldn't it make sense that there's a connection with the concept of how the 'universe says yes?'

Years of seeking had to—at some point—result in finding. Finding a living, breathing, and plausible framework of time and space to result in my here and now excites me.

This wasn't a fast or overnight conclusion. At first glance, it sounded too easy. And at times, it felt too hard. It might even go against what we were taught. Many are taught that life is hard, the rich get richer, we need better education, a better body, or that people with money are not good. Many are taught that we must accept our condition within the boundaries we are given and that some people are just lucky, while others are not. Many are taught the scarcity mindset, so they conserve or hoard. For others, it seems everything they touch turns to gold.

The process of reprogramming our minds to an abundant mindset requires a long and emotional look back on our lives in new ways. Whether we are journeying literally to visit a different country or to a life of abundance, it is not a passive journey, nor is it a solo journey.

We are actively participating in that journey and are also the very ones who are calling it forth. We are creating it.

"What You Seek is Seeking You."
~ Rumi

I decided to devote my personal life to this work as if it was as important as any career. I had an insatiable thirst for understanding our power to create in this free-will zone. It is the glass half empty or the glass half full. There is indeed a divine matrix that leads to an abundant life.

Vision boards. I know, I know. How many of us have made one and nothing happened? It's happened more than once that my vision boards resurfaced after cleaning out a closet--those magazine cut and pasted on images of what I thought I had wanted, everything from that personal love of my life soul-mate, healthy family relationships, trips around the world, and a beach home. These desires that no matter how many times in the past I cut and pasted on that poster board, would always end up back on the proverbial drawing board, instead.

So, I once again found myself making a vision board in 2015 with a group of friends. I pulled out a new sheet of poster board, grabbed some scissors, tape, and magazines and started dreaming. Once again, those same desires went back on the board. Once again, there were images of hearts, a loving couple holding hands, families laughing, travel and pictures of sand, kayaks, paddle boards, and palm trees. This time I was determined to really do this!

With each desire on that board, there was a stirring of excitement in my soul! Then something strange would happen to that feeling. Through awareness, I realized each time I thought of what I wanted, the good feelings would slowly shift from excitement to anxiety. How would I travel without an income to support that travel lifestyle? Who would go with me since I don't want to go alone? How would I give up my freedom to partner with a husband, when certainly there would be conflict, sacrifice, arguments, and disappointment? Heck, he might even snore! How would I ever be able to afford that beach home? I didn't have the cash to outright buy one or income to qualify for a loan, much less afford the upkeep of two homes. How?

I was continuing to choose feelings of paralysis by the how. Had my entire life been stuck on "how?!" Was that why those exciting feelings would dissipate like the condensation trail of a jet liner of desire? The desire was launched, but the negative feelings would override the good ones, until I was once again feeling less hope. I prayed harder. And worked harder. And kept staring blankly at my vision board, working hard to erase my feelings of doubt. And then I heard this voice in my head.

"The how is none of your business...."
Casey Plouffe, 7 Figure Network Marketer and Author

Ah, that's right! All I needed to do was not think about the how or what I didn't want! I must only think of, speak of, and hold onto those feelings of excitement. I only needed to feel how it would feel if what I wanted had already happened! Ok! Got it! How many times and in how many ways do I need to be reminded? Apparently, a lot!

As the winter months closed in and I stared at the beach images on my vision board daily, all I could think about was being on a beach. I thought of friends with beach homes. I even reached out to a few acquaintances to invite myself for the weekend. Ha, no takers; they barely knew me. Scrolling through the real estate listings for beach homes along the North and South Carolina coastlines became my favorite hobby. At least I was taking action, and that satisfied me quite nicely. This small action kept the feeling of 'act as if' at a happier level. If there was a beach home waiting for me, why not let the universe put it in front of me while I enjoyed scrolling through all possibilities?

"Act. As. If. Do not think about 'the how' and or those high-priced beach homes. Keep seeing yourself on the beach, Belinda," I would repeatedly tell myself.

A few months later, as the spring season approached, my friend Libby called.

"Belinda, my friend Gail is interested in your health coaching. But she wants to know if you can come to her beach home since that's where she's spending the next couple of weeks. Think you could do that?"

"Beach home?" I repeated. I now understood a dog's world. Ball? Did you say ball? Go out? Go bye bye? Did you say 'treat?' YES! I'd love to help your friend!

And just like that I found myself at her most adorable little beach condo tucked away on the famous salt marshes of the South Carolina coast, in what I later learned was America's

Oldest Seaside Resort, Pawleys Island and Litchfield Beach, SC.

While at Gail's, I would slip away for a walk through the jungle-like foot path to make my way over to the island beach. As my toes hit the sand and my body absorbed the roar of the ocean, with salty wind licking my face, there came a mighty flood of raw emotion. I could barely contain myself. Tears of gratitude and love swelled in my heart the size of that ocean. I will never forget the first time I stood at the inlet point between the two islands, soaking it all in, declaring, knowing, and proclaiming out loud right then and there as tears streamed down my face that somehow, someway, someday, I would own a home here. And the 'how' did not matter to me. I knew. I had found the beach I was meant to be on.

Scouring the real estate listings for the next few months became even more exciting as I continued to drill down to this place I was already calling home. Then, lo and behold, another call came. It was a blues musician acquaintance from Utah who asked if I'd be comfortable attending a family wedding with him in South Carolina. He needed a plus one.

"Of course I will!' I answered. "Where exactly in SC is it?"

'Hmmm, not sure. It's called Litchfield Beach. Have you heard of it?"

"Ha! Have I heard of it!? Yes! It's about four hours from where I live and you're not going to believe this. I was just there. I love the place! It's the exact beach I was on a few months ago, where I declared I'd one day own a home! How crazy is this?!"

My friend came. The wedding was phenomenal, and off we went to explore the area. We made our way to the famous

Murrells Inlet Marsh Walk, a few miles up the road from Litchfield Beach. There were open air restaurants, musicians, and artists. One artist in particular really grabbed my attention. He was painting coastal and beach themed art on plywood sheets, live and on the spot, as the tourists and I watched spell bound by his craft. The minute I saw his $20 whimsical blue crab painting, I knew I had to buy it for my new home. So, I did! And I also bought lots of coastal themed jewelry handmade by a lady named Shug, a local fan favorite. Before I knew it, Shug and I were friends. Months later, I found myself staying for a week at Shug's home on more than one occasion!

By now, almost a year had passed since I first visited Gail, but it didn't feel like a year. I loved my painting, the jewelry, and my newfound friends, and turtles. Yes, turtles started showing up. In airport displays or public restrooms on wallpaper, turtle art was appearing in the strangest places it seemed. Even my mom gave me a wooden turtle carving! I was perplexed; what's with all these turtles?! Only time would tell. But I knew there was a connection!

I know for sure that when we hold onto our dreams and desires, pay attention to our feelings! Rather than cancelling the receiving of our desires by questioning 'how,' instead hold onto the feeling of having received them! Everything, and I mean *everything* that shows up, is not a coincidence or random. Enjoy the wisdom expressed in your feelings as they are important pieces to your abundance! And I love a good puzzle!

"Coincidences are God's way of remaining anonymous."
~ Albert Einstein

Then came that day I received an email alert that a condo had come on the market in my very low price range. Guess where it was? You got it! It was in the exact same community I had visited a year before, where Gail lived!

"Joyce, how are you?! Hey, what are you doing this weekend, I know it's short notice but come ride to the beach with me; there's a condo I want to look at!"

"Uh, ok, where we going?!"

I hung up the phone, giddy with excitement. We had a plan. There's nothing like a good friend who'll jump in a car at a moment's notice for a girl's beach weekend! We found a great little hotel room and off to the beach we went!

An offer was made! This was it! I knew I had found the one! I went low, so low I thought I had almost lost my chance but held onto the belief I was to have this property. They came back, I came back, and before I knew it, they accepted my cash offer!

"CASH? Are you crazy? You don't have that kind of cash laying around, do you?" my friend asked.

"No, I don't, but I'll figure it out! I just know I'm supposed to have this place. It'll all work out!"

The following week I would lay awake trying to figure out the money. Where would I find this cash? How could I borrow it? Who would trust me, and how would I repay it? And with feelings of excitement, I'd then release those questions to the sand man, and get a good night's sleep.

One morning I woke up with total clarity! Ah ha! I had the answer! I made a few phone calls, and bam, the deals were cut. A few weeks later, the home was mine!

I did it! We did it. We all did it! The random events and people were not random at all! They were synchronistic!

17

syn·chro·nism (sĭng′krə-nĭz′əm, sĭn′-) n.

1. Coincidence in time; simultaneousness.

2. A chronological listing of historical personages or events so as to indicate parallel existence or occurrence.

3. Representation in the same artwork of events that occurred at different times.

Then came furnishings. Who cares!? Who needs furniture? I had a roof, a hot shower, a kitchen, and a floor. I brought a plate, a few cups, some silverware, a camp chair, a pillow and blanket from my other home, and bought a $7 blow up mattress. I was the happiest I had ever been! Glamping indoors made me happy!

Every day I walked, ok not walked, I skipped with joy on that beach! I smiled and waved to everyone I passed. I started to recognize the faces of locals and we soon became friends. One day, a gentleman—whose name is John—stopped me on the beach and asked if I was new here. As we chatted, he pointed to his beach front condo and said he was in the process of remodeling and was going to get all new furniture and upgrades.

"Furniture," I repeated. "Did you say furniture? What are you going to do with your old furniture, if you don't mind me asking?"

"I'm giving it to Habitat for Humanity."

"Oh, wow, how generous of you! I know this may sound crazy, but can I come to look at it?"

"Sure! But you don't want this old furniture, I wouldn't think. I mean, there's nothing wrong with it; I'm just ready for new."

And a few months later, with a couple of new sofa pillows and a little cleaning, the furniture found itself fitting beautifully in my cozy little place as a stop over until such time as I release it to Habitat for Humanity. The crab artwork perfectly matched the paint color of the walls in the guest bedroom. And when I asked that same artist to paint another picture for me that would go with the beach theme of the area, guess what he delivered?

If you guessed a turtle painting, you are correct! A giant turtle painting! Little did I know that the South Carolina United Turtle Enthusiasts, aka "SCUTE" non-profit organization, was formed in 1990 in the Pawleys Island / Litchfield Beach community in response to the need for better protection of sea turtles that nest here and on the SC coastline.

Traditionally, the turtle is symbolic of the way of peace, whether it's inviting us to cultivate peace of mind or a peaceful relationship with our environment. It is also a sign that wherever you are, you are at home. Your home is where your heart is.

I have peace of mind, I am grounded, and I am in a relationship with my environment, my God, my soul, my heart, and my universe. The magic of synchronicity is one we experience every day, whether we realize it or not.

By the way, within eight months of the condo purchase, another property I had owned and tried to sell for years, finally sold! Personal loans on the condo were paid off, and the positive feelings of experiences I desired continue to come forth. The friends, boating, beach picnics, connections, and blessings multiply to this day. I could tell you story after story, but instead, I want you to write your own.

Know this for sure: whatever you desire, whatever you call forth and really want, when you act as if you already have it and feel those good feelings, start to look for it, because it has shown up. In fact, events, people, and conditions will keep showing up over and over, time and time again, in so many ways, that had you only connected the dots, you would have had it a lot sooner. Hold onto your good feelings! Know what you truly want because 'the how' to achieving it is none of your business! That's the fun part! All things will come together in ways you could have never imagined!

"Now faith is the substance of things hoped for, the evidence of things not seen."
Hebrews 11:1

One last thought. After an email closing on the condo in April 2016, that glorious day came that I drove four hours to get the keys and take possession of my dream. Upon arriving, I parked the car, stepped out, took a deep breath, and smiled. What a feeling!

About that time, a lady came out from the unit below mine. She had the biggest and best smile of anyone I had ever seen!!

"Hello! I'm Belinda, and I just bought this place," I said to her as I pointed to the upstairs condo above the one she just came out of. "I'm from Greenville, SC, and this will be my beach home. I'm so excited!"

"Wow!" she answered. My name is Anna, and I, too, own a home in the Greenville area! And this is my beach home! So nice to meet you!"

It was just one more confirmation that I was exactly where I was supposed to be. And Anna and I have been best friends ever since!

So it was that moment when I was challenged with putting words onto paper that Anna stepped out of her condo on a chilly January day in 2021 and suggested that I start by writing

down three words or phrases that made me think of abundance.

> Anna's smile....it's as big as the ocean

> The beach....is where I find the ocean

> Act as if....I am the ocean

God bless you all, and may you know exactly what you want,
because the *seachronistic* path to having it...is the easiest part
of the journey.

"ABUNDANCE IS A PROCESS OF LETTING GO; THAT WHICH IS EMPTY CAN RECEIVE."

~ Bryant H. McGill

CHAPTER TWO

Abundance is a State of Mind

By John Spender

A bundant living is an alignment as much as it's having money in your bank account. It's a way of being, and it starts with feeling abundant.

Knowing and feeling abundant is the shield that will protect you from the limiting beliefs that everyone is exposed to sooner or later. Beliefs like; Money doesn't grow on trees. We can't afford it. Do you think I'm made of money? You have to work hard for money. Money is the root of all evil. Rich people are criminals. You have to have money to make money. Do any of these sound familiar? The fear of not being abundant is passed down from generation to generation all over the globe. So many people constantly worry about how they are going to pay the rent. Where is the money going to come from? They ask themselves questions like, *Why can't I get a better job? Why can't I earn more money? Why can't I be successful? Why can't I get ahead? Why am I always broke?* These disempowering questions only reinforce the 'lack' paradigm that most of us find ourselves in at some point in time. But do we really want the solution? Are we keen to do something about it? Do we want to break the paradigm of lack, limitation, and poverty that has plagued many of our families for centuries?

Who wouldn't say yes, right? Over the following pages, I will share principles that I have learned which have guided me to live life abundantly. Moreover, if you apply them, you will get the same result as surely as the night turns into day. Maybe you already have a lot of money, but you don't feel like you have enough or fear losing it. Both are part of the same hamburger; they are at opposite ends but are still the same. Living abundantly isn't something that comes naturally for most people. I remember my parents separating when I was just five years old and my mom found herself with three little people to care for, clothe, and feed. It was a challenging time for her, and she adopted the mindset of work hard and save. After living on our grandparent's farm for a year, we moved into a house with holes in the floorboards and wore second-hand clothes from The Salvation Army. From the outside looking in, things may have seemed bleak, but we were okay.

Our grandparents had bought us, three kids, a Disney plaster mold kit which consisted of Micky Mouse, Donald Duck, and Goofy. My brother, being the eldest, poured the molds with the plaster and, when set, would take the molds off and paint them. The tricky part was taking the molds off. Adam was good at handling Micky and Donald, but Goofy's nose would always break off. Once we had several painted statues, we set up a table out in front of our rental house situated on a main road with a footpath. Our first business was ready to roll. Being six with blonde hair and blue eyes, I was good at charming old ladies. They thought I was cute and would buy one of the Disney characters. In less than two hours, I had sold all of our stock. I wanted to repeat the process and buy more plaster, but my brother, three years older, bought lollies and slime o. Although our first business didn't last long, I learned a valuable lesson about abundance being a state of mind. As children, we didn't see ourselves as poor or different from anyone else. We saw an opportunity, tapped into our resourcefulness, and money couldn't wait to jump into our pockets or my brother's pocket.

Abundance is all around us once we notice its presence; tapping into the limitless supply becomes much easier. Spreading this awareness is what my fellow coauthors and I plan to do with this book. Let's share an awareness of abundance throughout the world like wildfire, a fire that will banish fear, lack, and want from your life. This awareness is the source of all success, wealth, empowerment, and material gain. The awareness of abundance will draw all to you: a new phone, career, partner, whatever your heart desires. Your wish is your command when connected to this invisible substance that connects all who cultivate its presence. It is omnipresent and so powerful, magnetizing everything in your life to vibrate in harmony with it, dispelling every unwanted condition. If you are lost in a maze of false beliefs, this idea will elevate your experience. If you are in the poor zone, it will take you out. If you are financially down on your luck, it will reach down and pick you up. If you have hit rock bottom, it will take you to the top. If your faith is weak, it will fortify your resolve.

Aligning your attitude with abundance will amplify your income, bring riches, activate good, attract opportunities, cancel debts, stimulate business, prevent failure, nourish your aspiration, clarify vision, generate peace, heal wounds, solve problems, expand imagination, return losses, eliminate hardship, remove blocks, dispel fear, squash worry, shut down doubt, integrate the mind, raise your self-esteem, loosen tensions, and open doors. This energy is your Aladdin's lamp to infinite abundance in every area of your life. This isn't some sort of a-ra-ra rally or exaggerated motivational speech. I'm speaking from experience, having lived through many ups and downs. I've had an on and off-again relationship with abundance almost all of my life. One particular time, I started expanding my online coaching practice into Singapore, hosting live events every month. I live in Bali and barely made enough money to cover my flights, accommodation, and expenses.

Due to a lack of belief in my abilities, the venture lasted a year before I had to admit defeat and cut my losses.

I had lost my connection with abundance consciousness and found myself downgrading in Bali, which was quite embarrassing for me to face and sit with my failure. It was challenging to feel abundant when the outside world told me that I wasn't. Firstly, I developed a strong morning routine consisting of yoga, affirmations, meditation, and fresh fruits for breakfast. This helped me to shift the way I saw my reality with a primary focus on income-producing activities. I also gave myself ample time to daydream, creating a vision board and my own counsel after reading Napoleon Hills *Think and Grow Rich*. An idea came into my awareness of making a film, which seemed crazy as I had no money at the time. I modeled Hill's success of having imaginary conversations with his counsel. As he had indicated, the conversations I was having started to feel real, almost like a form of telepathy. I began to feel more abundant when one of my nightly imagery conversations with Dr. Micheal Beckwith felt unbelievably real. I explained the vision for the movie documentary to the council, and Micheal spoke up as if he was in the room with me. It was almost like a shout when he said he loved the vision and wanted to feature in the film. I ask him how? His response was short and simple and filled me with confidence, "Come over to Agape (his center), and we will make it happen."

"I am abundant" is an affirmation I repeated over and over again. I planned to reach out to as many thought leaders in the personal development space as I could and offer them a spot in the film with the promise of securing some big names like Dr. Michael Beckwith and Jack Canfield. I raised enough money to fly myself and a videographer to Los Angeles, filming Beckwith, Canfield, Lisa Garr, Dr. John DeMartini, and more guests over four years. I'm on the last stretch of funding the live acting scenes at the present moment.

I discovered that thoughts are seeds that come to us from anywhere and everywhere as they float through the air looking for the right mental soil. The suitable ground is a part of our awareness. Just as a vegetable garden must be free from weeds to thrive, our minds need to be free from negativity, opposing contradictory thoughts and limiting beliefs to succeed in connecting with abundance and in becoming abundance. The problem is not with the seed but with the soil. You must remove the impediments of fear, worry, and doubt, and then the idea of abundance can take root and grow to maturity. The unseen becomes seen, starting from nothingness and rising to the manifested. Therefore, cultivating the soil of the heart, mind, and soul takes us from lack and moves us into the fertile grounds of prosperity and abundance.

Firstly, do you know what you desire? Do you know what you deserve? A new apartment? More money or better health? Well, plant your idea into the fertile medium of the subconscious. Plant it deep and cultivate it with recognition and belief, fertilize it with focus and concentration, and nurture it with faith and appreciation, all while activating it with your consciousness. If you will only condition your beingness, there is nothing that you can't bring into existence. You are an unlimited being that can create anything that you desire.

You are the universe, and the universe is you. When you enter the universe's consciousness, connecting with its intelligence, you effectively tap into all that is and ever was created. The channeler Esther Hicks communicates this through the entity Abraham using the term to enter the vortex of creation. Jesus calls it the Kingdom of Heaven. Suppose we abide in this abundance consciousness and expand our awareness, keeping our thoughts pure and our beingness true to its frequency.

Simply allow the divine substance to momentarily shape itself around our thoughts as they materialize into our lives in those things we think and focus on. Moreover, we must keep our minds off our troubles and instead centered in the universal intelligence of pure consciousness — abundance consciousness.

It served me well to repeat the affirmation: *I am abundance.* I invite you to say the words with emotion and feel them with your heart. Stake your claim and know your worth. Think abundance throughout the day, for that in which you honor will be honored. Think plenty all the time and watch it manifest in your life in all its forms. You may be wondering, *How can I think of abundance all the time?* You do it by making it the primary foundation from which all other words stem. Ralph Waldo Emerson said, "Man is what he thinks about all day long." See abundance in the flowers and the rows of stacked shelves filled with endless goods. See it in the night sky with the bountiful stars shining bright. Feel it in nature through magnificent trees. At any given moment, we are surrounded by abundance. Can you see it?

What is your main focus? Your thought pattern is the matrix or the fixed mold by which all other thoughts pass. Worry usually starts as a slight fear in the mind and becomes basic or habitual through repetition. We repeat the same worry day after day until it becomes a habit or an automatic expression. Patterns make a channel or a path through which our thoughts and deeds travel. The channel enlarges as the idea is repeated, getting deeper and wider until the habit tends to influence all our thoughts, actions, and beingness. This is why we are what we think about all day long. If someone's basic thought foundation is worry, everything in her life will be tainted by the specter of anxiety, fear, lack of courage, indecisiveness, coyness, and lack of confidence.

Our most dominant thought is like a chili paste that Indonesians add to their food, adding heat to everything they eat. Here is a person who has allowed the basic worry thought to permeate his consciousness. Worry thoughts will affect everything in this person's life, spicing all other thoughts with worry. The whole spectrum of negative emotions will stick to it like flies to flypaper. Others will sense the pessimistic mental atmosphere and will be repelled by it. No matter how good or how desirable one's products or services may be, as long as he carries this frequency with him, he will repel his goodness instead of attracting it.

You've heard about the atmosphere of homes, restaurants, buildings, towns, and communities being made up of the collective consciousness of the people who live there. A man's consciousness is related directly to his thoughts, beliefs, and habits—often subtly seeping out in the things he says and does—that reveal him to others. If his primary thought is poverty or lack, others will know it and treat him accordingly. When I began to surround myself with the imagery council of thought leaders, people like Jack Canfield, Michael Bernard Beckwith, Tony Robbins, Dr. Wayne Dyer, Lisa Garr, Alan Cohen, Rhonda Burn, Dr. John Demartini, and many more, their pictures stuck to a vision board, my consciousness began to shift, and the synchronicities related to my desires manifested quickly. I mentioned earlier that after consistent meetings with my committee, the imagery conversations felt real. I spoke to a friend's husband about what I was doing with myself. Casually mentioning the vision for the film project, he told me that he knew Jack Canfield and Dr. John Demartini. He would gladly introduce me if he could share his message in the film. That's when the music from the twilight zone sounded in my head.

How then should we approach and change these established destructive habits of thinking? By choosing to embrace a magnanimous beingness towards all life, fully embodying and adapting the new paradigm, you wish to create. Let's fill our awareness with thoughts of assurances, poise, faith, self-confidence, serenity, and inner determination. Allow yourself to transform by surrounding yourself with an atmosphere of success, achievement, and strength of character. Permit yourself to radiate qualities of fearlessness, inner peace, trust, optimism, and self-reliance. When we do this, we attract the best from everything, everybody, and synchronicities become the norm. Before you know it, you will inspire confidence and compel attention. Believing in yourself will inspire confidence in others. The new paradigm shift will release universal intelligence into consciousness and change your life's color, character, and tone. Instead of worry, you will generate faith. This is precisely what happened to me, and it can work for you too. Living abundantly is indeed a mindset, a way of being that anyone can champion.

The question is, how do you stop yourself from slipping into the primary thought of worry? You do so deliberately and persistently, taking a new pattern of confidence and appreciation into your lifestyle. It all boils down to our habits of thinking. When I lost faith and trust in my abilities during my Singapore venture, I slipped into a pattern of thinking that there wasn't enough money to make things happen when, in fact, the missing ingredients were self-belief and innovation to create something different. Having a sense of awareness was the first step in changing my point of focus. The nature of habit is an interesting one, moving along the lines of least resistance. This is highlighted clearly by Edward E Beals in his book *The Law of Financial Success* when he states, "If you have to walk over a field or through a forest, you know how natural it is for you to choose the clearest path over the less worn one. And greatly in preference to stepping out across the field or through the woods to form a new path."

Patterns are formed through repetition and are developed by an observable natural law in all animate, and some would say inanimate things. Once a piece of paper is folded in a particular way, it will fold along the same lines next time. Nature is the best example of this. Notice how rivers and streams of water cut their courses through the land and therefore flow along effortlessly. The law of least resistance is in effect everywhere. It's like the indents in a record the needle follows. If we don't like the tune we are creating, we must scratch the record.

One way to eradicate the old process of worry is to form a bigger concept of confidence. As a confident thought grows, the mental path of concern will gradually fill up from disuse. The old path will grow less and less distinct until it eventually disappears. Do you see why changing habits of thought is so essential to expanding your awareness of abundance? When you know how to change your predominant thoughts, you know how to change everything in your life. You are well on the way to something better and more aligned to the consciousness of universal intelligence, your higher self.

In the initial phase of changing habits, allow patience, persistence, and trust to be your guiding light. The stars don't disappear in daylight hours. They merely disappear from one's sight, but they are still there, shining bright as in the night. You will see results when your new conscious credo becomes deeper and more robust than the old unconscious ones. Once the new pattern is outlined and adopted, with immense certainty and feeling for it to take hold. You must make it the intimate and vital predominating ever-living quality of your being, immersing your consciousness in the new paradigm.

As discussed earlier, affirmations are the rock of support that I needed to reshape my reality. They gave me the necessary self-confidence to birth the council for my film. I would say to myself: *I am confident. I am abundant. I am grateful. I am a success. I picture abundance for myself and others; I always have more money coming in than going out. I give generously to myself and others* and many more. Feel what you say—feel it deeply with all your heart and with great joy. Dwell on your statements until they firmly synchronize with your emotional nervous system. There are several rules that I follow to embody new affirmations of thought and beingness.

1. Every time I caught myself using the old-habit path of lack, I celebrated the mental catch and mostly repeated the simple affirmation that *I'm abundance and everything is always working out for me.*

2. As much as I could, I kept my thoughts changed out of the negative path and held and affirmed positive thoughts. If you slip, celebrate, and come back to your new affirmation: *I am abundance, and everything is always working out for me.* Allow simplicity to be your guiding force.

3. I energized the new thought-action (affirmations) with hope, power, belief, conviction, and determination when I expressed them.

4. I made my new pattern clear, strong, profound, and as positive as I could.

5. Consistency was my secret weapon. I would repeat my affirmations three times a day to ingrain a new mental path into my subconscious mind. Repetition is the answer to forming new habits of any kind.

The objective we want to accomplish is two-fold: to eradicate the offending thought pattern of doubt and to drop a new idea into the pool of subconscious cerebration so that the new un-hindered thought can take form in the creative substance that is the nucleus of abundance. The law of abundance is already within our hearts, subtly pressing the mind to act. Our job is to release it for our daily needs, to open channels for its expression.

Don't hold the idea; let the idea hold you! Do you feel me? This is crucial to your success. Do not affirm unless the corresponding emotion supports your affirmation. This is where many people come unstuck, as they don't understand this principle. We display our good by first connecting with the universe's intelligence and not through parroting affirmations or mouthing declarations without feeling. The law of attraction responds to us by correlating our states of mind and our hearts' essence. It operates through our mental equivalent or beliefs. If your heart isn't in it, you are not connected with the source. When the principle of abundance is set in motion through affirmation and acceptance, the law of attraction operates through us.

Why must the new thought pattern be housed in the present tense? Why do we say *I am abundance* instead of saying *I will be abundant*? Why must we state something we do not have? Life always works in the present moment by direct affirmation. I will be abundant and good, is putting our abundance off until some future time. To affirm our good in the present is to cause it to appear. Law plus acceptance plus belief in the pattern. If the idea for abundance is to become a superpower in our lives, we must inwardly accept it as a present fact. Our thought, will, and imagination must agree with what we say. We must banish all fear of lack from our desire. A turning point for me was loving and trusting my imagination to allow my desires to flow freely. This happened immediately after the failure in Singapore, and it began with affirmations and sitting still in meditation. Reading Napoleon Hills' *Think and Grow Rich* gave me the idea of creating a vision board filled with pictures of my council and sharing the desire to create the film with them first.

Now I'm going to ask you to start building your basic thought pattern for abundance without further delay. Center your thought again in our affirmation *I am abundance*. This is the nucleus that is to grow and multiply indefinitely. It must be backed up with your persistent faith and desire. Your idea of abundance might be a better position, more income, a nice holiday, a compatible partner, or increased health. The law of attraction says you can have anything you desire, and if you believe you already have it—that is, if you have the objective acceptance of the thing desired, then it is yours to live into.

Now contemplate that for a few moments. Not the money to meet the mortgage, not the new car, not the new house, but the basic idea *I am abundance*. If you accept my invitation, you're going to change your consciousness out of the old mold of lack and into the new paradigm of plenty. You will create a unique habit atmosphere, a new thought inclination, and a new state of beingness. That is your significant responsibility. We will start this idea of abundance revolving on its axis at such an elevated rate of speed that it will draw into our lives all the good things we need. We will boost your consciousness to recognize not only monetary abundance but abundance matching any of our desires. If you desire more self-esteem, you will meet many people that operate from a high level and elevate you by proximity.

The rest of the process is a matter of sustained attention, faith, feeling, acting, and seeing. See the new idea clearly, realize it, feel it, and accept it. Speed it up with your belief, keep it alive with your faith, feed it with fresh, rich, powerful life-giving images. Give it motion through action, act it out: *I am abundance.* Discover how rich you are. Keep the abundance idea circulating freely through your mind. See it generating prosperity, opportunities, and success. Do not allow negative thoughts to creep in and sabotage your divine good. *I am abundance.* Keep repeating it until it goes underground and takes form. *I am abundance.* Feel its frequency. Rejoice in it. Bless it. Love it. Accelerate the rate of vibration by telling your subconscious mind that you are already abundant. Act as if with a mindset of deep appreciation.

If you desire abundance, don't say I want to get rid of poverty; be affirmative and positive. Say what you mean, and mean what you say. If your thought is filled with the idea of getting rid of lack, you are increasing lack in your consciousness. Make your primary thought one of prosperity, opulence, plenty, and wealth. Think and speak of nothing else. Oh, yes, I know the rent is due, and you have a lot of unpaid bills, but you are not going to think of these right now. You are going to think abundance, know abundance, feel plenty and nothing else. You're going to etch abundance so deeply into your awareness that nothing else can come into your life. That is what we mean by building a new mental equivalent. It's creating a new basic thought out of impulsion that will flood your life with good. It is making a new path for God by getting everything out of her way. It takes everything that isn't perfection from out of your consciousness, trading it in for something better and more desirable.

Our desires must be definite and flexible, and we should always expect something better than what we have set our hearts on. The purpose of our desires is to open our consciousness so that we can use the expanded form, enlarging our connection to Source. See it as a process of evolving your consciousness.

It is the nature of abundance consciousness to outdo itself. The gift is to attain a new state of expansion. When we start to connect with this higher consciousness, we clear the invisible channels to become visible. When our abundance is the outward growth of a rich consciousness, it is satisfying, permanent, and secure. Our job is to raise our vibration and feel worthy enough to receive, thereby creating a new state of beingness.

The value of repetition cannot be emphasized enough. It's like the constant dripping of water on a stone leaving its mark. The continuous repetition of your affirmation fuses it with the subconscious mind and therefore materializes the idea. Embody the idea to the extent that you feel that you are always abundantly provided for while following your path in life. I challenge you to break the cycle of lack, scarcity, shortage, and want that has plagued human beings for centuries. Create a timeline from your very first memory of feeling abundant to the most recent one and every year in-between. Allow about two hours of your time to sit and reflect on all the plentiful moments in your life. Can you remember the first time you earned money? What about having an oversupply of food? Or your first family vacation? Recall the times when you felt most abundant and watch the increase begin to manifest into your life even more.

As you embrace the mindset of abundance, know that you are breaking generational beliefs that there is a limited supply of all things. Letting go of these limiting beliefs is like healing a virus, and it can take time and determination. Out with worry and in with plenty, enough for all. I would like to thank you for spending the last 15-20 minutes with me, and I encourage you to reread this chapter as many times as needed. I recommend that you seek the more rooted blessings found in abundant living, as well as the gratification it brings to such a worthwhile endeavor. God bless you, my friend, as you depend on abundance consciousness for all you will ever need, and abundance consciousness never ceases to deliver.

**"ABUNDANCE IS NOT SOMETHING WE ACQUIRE.
IT IS SOMETHING WE TUNE INTO."**

~Wayne Dyer

CHAPTER THREE

Lessons Learned in Abundant Living

By Abhinav Gupta

T he morning was sunny and clear, dressed in the fresh warmth of June. It was still early for work, but staff had started entering the office building. We had a whole floor, and the steadily increasing humming of my employees echoed within its walls. They were greeting one another and exchanging ideas on how to complete their tasks at hand. I'd arrived earlier than usual today as I needed to prepare for the signing of a deal with a new client, a big one, so I was able to witness the growing bustle. I relished the sound because it captured the synergy running through the veins of my business—the call center I'd put up three years ago and had been nurturing ever since. The stir certainly had a ring of long-term success to it.

The client, Peter, a senior manager of the mortgage accreditor who was looking to run a new campaign, arrived, and we began the closed-door transaction at my office. I'd given my receptionist, Christina, explicit do-not-disturb instructions at any point during the meeting, since this account could place our contact center at the forefront of the industry.

Peter and I were having an insightful conversation leading up to a smooth signing process when Christina barged into the room. The disruption almost made me mad as a cut snake, but before I could react, I saw Christina's ashen face. I politely excused myself from Peter to deal with whatever situation was developing outside. There in the foyer, four smug men faced me in a way that said I should be intimidated. They introduced themselves as representatives of some liquidation company and, without further do, demanded that I cease operations, get everyone to vacate the premises, and allow them to take control of my company. Immediately!

'Wait, liquidation, what?!' I had a million questions but was too nonplussed; I couldn't even open my mouth. My tongue refused to utter a word, and my mind went numb. My vision blurred, although I was able to make out the four strange male figures that had begun sauntering across the building floor. They were now behaving like they owned the office, like it was they—not I—who had passed many meal-less days and spent countless insomniac nights building the company from the ground up. In the ensuing seconds, I felt my business collapsing, and my world came crashing down. Suddenly, everything became dark.

Not sure if anyone in my circle had ever dealt with liquidators; I certainly never had! With the coming of those smug men, everyone was ordered to leave, and a padlock was put on our office doors. My valued company and personal bank accounts were frozen. I couldn't withdraw a single cent and didn't even have $20 to fill my car with petrol! I had no idea how to deal with this unexpected mess. Who should I share this problem with, and who would help me solve it? What else could a 23-year-old man be experiencing in his life?

The sense of not being in control of anything made me panic. I stood at the roadside by my building helplessly, looking like a man who'd never had anything in life. I gazed at the passers-by and found each one of them to be superior to me. It was Friday. As the hours passed, the pubs and clubs started to light up and buzz with excitement and joy. Yet here I was, devastated as though a ton of bricks had piled onto me.

* * *

As I write this chapter, I harken back to those years of my journey and all the experiences I've had. I can fairly say that I've changed as a person—indeed, I've changed a lot. The truth is, I was a complete loser back then.

In school, I was hardworking but not exactly competent; it was always an arduous task to achieve even average grades. I was resigned to the fact that my life was horrible. I didn't have friends. I had no social life, no hobbies, no independence, no confidence, no charisma, no sense of humor, no sense of purpose. Basically, I had nothing except for my desire for abundant wealth. Why? Because I thought that this was abundant living. I carried this notion for a while until I realized that wealth was a mere by-product of the person that I was.

Fast forward 16 years, and I have taken a 180-degree turn. I'm now a different person, no longer a complete loser. What happened?

This is my story, which I hope you will benefit from.

My name is Abhinav, but people call me Abhi, which is shorter and easier to pronounce. I was nine when my family emigrated from our homeland to Melbourne, Australia. The day we arrived, it was chilly and cold. It was mostly raining, and the whole place was wet.

My father came to Australia with only a suitcase. It was a time of recession, and employment was extremely difficult to come by. Dad was a civil engineer, but he struggled to find a job in his field. He delivered pizza in the evening to make ends meet. My mum, younger brother, and I joined him in distributing flyers, a gig that supplemented our meagre household income. We were so broke that my parents would argue late at night about the bills or who spent the extra $20. I saw my family go through the toughest times.

It was a tough time for me because people my age treated me as nothing but an alien in this new country. I tried to make new friends in school, but I ended up being called names and being teased. I withdrew to myself and just focused on business subjects to pursue my dream of being in business—even if it was against my parents' wishes. Dad and Mum wanted me to become an accountant, lawyer, doctor, or engineer.

After finishing high school in 1999, I set up my first business call center and sales/marketing company from my bedroom. I was awarded my first-ever sales contract through Jim's Alarm, an established company. My client would be ADT Security, another respected name in the field. The tasks included setting appointments over the phone and coming face-to-face with prospective buyers of alarm and security systems.

At night, I was studying to complete my degree in information technology. I had no interest in IT, but I had to keep Dad off my back and Mum stoked. Time came when my family and I had the basic things we needed: food, clothing, a roof over our heads. We even had a bit of luxury sometimes. Life was no longer bad. But it still felt that way to me.

The biggest problems showed up in my late twenties. I was finally making decent money, with my company signing on to different sales contracts that meant huge profits. I could eat out whenever I wanted to and buy whatever I fancied. I drove a decent car. Despite this, I was as miserable as a bandicoot. I felt inadequate. I had a scarcity mindset.

If I had less than $2,000 in my bank account, I got massive anxiety and literally couldn't sleep. Even when things were going very well, and I was making the most money I'd ever made, I believed that everything I possessed was never enough. It didn't matter that I was earning loads of money. I couldn't seem to feel at peace with the fact that what I already owned or was due to come my way, sufficed. My trepidation was never-ending; it pushed me into a black hole. Unsurprisingly, I attracted people, circumstances, and events that matched my subconscious fear. I suffered unexpected injuries that led to costly medical bills. My car kept breaking down. My company's sales stopped coming. We were losing contracts. There was a common thread, and it matched the same feeling I had as a kid witnessing my parents fight over money—or the lack of it.

Things changed when I met Paul, the man who would enlighten me about the law of attraction (LOA). I'd heard of things like the best-selling book *The Secret*, which hinged on this LOA philosophy, but these didn't quite click for me on a deep level...until Paul, my mentor, broke it down to a science I could grasp. He showed me the beliefs and subconscious programming that caused problematic situations no matter how hard I worked.

I enlisted Paul's help, and we spent days rewiring my subconscious mind around money, making sales, creating wealth, receiving abundance, and related matters. The results were shocking. At the time, I was in business coaching and mentoring, and over the next three months, my income jumped up by 90%. But the weird part was, I wasn't working any harder. All I did was make certain changes in my attitude towards life to attract wealthy-minded people who were only too happy to pay me for my professional services. Soon after applying Paul's teachings, my life was turned around for the better. The injuries and medical bills stopped coming. My car started playing nice. My company's sales rolled back in. We won more contracts than we'd lost. Best of all, I was no longer that person who felt inadequate. I was no longer burdened with the scarcity mindset.

* * *

If there's anything to take from my journey, it's this: You can struggle to change your external circumstances, but until you do something about your subconscious programming and mindset, nothing's going to change for good.

And if you're challenged with a scarcity mentality, which is detrimental in every aspect of life, here are the sure-fire steps to take in doing a 180-degree turn towards its antithesis—the abundance mindset:

Step 1: **Believe you can do it.**

'The mind is everything,' goes Buddha's teaching. 'What you think, you become.'

If you wish to feel adequate, to feel like you are and have enough, then tell yourself over and over that it's quite possible to turn this feeling into a reality. The world is your oyster, and having faith in yourself is the key to creating a marvelous pearl out of it.

Step 2: **Focus on getting there.**

You want an abundance mindset? Map your route towards it! Ask yourself what would make you feel satisfied and content, then take stock of your capabilities and utilize these wisely in order to reach that state.

If your goal seems too high to achieve, break it down into more attainable targets that will become your stepping stones. Make an inventory of available resources—your time, energy, passion, talent, skill, physical tools. No matter how scant your resources are, channel these on hitting one target after another, so you can advance in the pursuit of your overarching goal.

What's important is, you believe in the first place that you can pursue your goal, that you certainly don't lack the desire and drive to reach it. Remember, it's the feeling of lack that feeds the scarcity mindset. So nurture the opposite and let hope flow with abandon.

Step 3: **Keep your eyes peeled for opportunities.**

An abundance mindset knows no bounds and has no limits. It opens your world to the bright prospects that a scarcity mindset has dimmed. So as you move along the path to your goal, train your sights on new things that can lead to brilliant ideas, awesome choices, and amazing possibilities. Seek ways to make these work to your advantage.

In case you stumble, get up and gain strength from this experience. Live by Confucius' words: 'Our greatest glory is not in never falling, but in rising every time we fall.'

Step 4: **Be in the company of individuals with an abundance mindset.**

'Birds of a feather flock together,' the proverb goes.

As you strive to rise from the ashes of a scarcity mindset, which reeks of negativity, endeavor to soar with people whose attitude brims with positivity. You can reach great heights faster this way because no one will weigh you down, belittle you, and say you're not enough.

Step 5: **Give of yourself.**

An abundance mindset is marked by satisfaction, contentment, a sense of fulfilment, and a feeling of fullness. People who carry it believe they are enough, not only for themselves but for others as well. They are magnanimous, and they can afford to share generously with those who lack.

Whenever you can, lend a helping hand. Just remember that giving of yourself isn't always about money or other material things. It could be about filling a lack in mind, heart, or spirit—like sharing a skill, a listening ear, a shoulder to cry on, or a few words of wisdom.

Step 6: **Show appreciation and gratitude.**

People with an abundance mindset recognize the good and are thankful for it. If you want to be among and like them, do as they do: Stop and smell the roses, count your blessings, and acknowledge the help of others at all times.

Once you start appreciating and being grateful for the wonderful things in, about, and around you, your outlook on the world and life itself will change for the better. Trust me, I know.

* * *

Why is an abundance mindset important?

The straightforward answer is this: An abundance mindset defines or redefines you as a person who is satisfied and content, with plenty to share—someone with the confidence and freedom to do a lot of good in life, for self and others.

With that confidence and freedom, along with positivity, you're bound to attract all the pleasant things you desire and expect, reach your goals, and help others along the way without feeling buggered.

If you want to attain the abundance mindset to attract wealth first and foremost, so be it. There's nothing wrong with that, as long as you're doing it legally and ethically. And if you're building your wealth as an entrepreneur, that's even better because you could be rewarded immensely for your creativity, ingenuity, and courage to ignite and kindle the fire in your belly—without having to deal with a corporate brass that can be very limiting.

Following my mentor's (Paul) steps towards the abundance mindset is just the beginning. You have to perform the steps over and over... and over again, in a rinse-and-repeat fashion, to succeed and continue succeeding. You may choose to go it alone, of course, although it involves risks: the risk of doing it incorrectly, the risk of doing it incompletely, and so forth. Or you may choose to enlist a mentor like Paul, who will proactively guide you through your journey as if he is your jolly ol' mate.

Here's a list of reasons why you need a mentor to achieve an abundant mindset and attain your wealth goals:

Reason 1: **A mentor is your breathing treasure-trove of knowledge, wisdom, and first-hand experience.**

Having been in a situation similar to yours and overcoming every difficulty tied to it, your mentor has got what it takes to guide you through your journey. He or she is your teacher and role model, who has studied, understood, and gone through the very steps being taught to you. Your mentor is your testament to the transformation of losers to winners.

Reason 2: **Your mentor provides a helping hand and a listening ear.**

Being of an abundant mindset and having attained wealth goals himself or herself, your mentor has the ability and determination to support you every step of the way. He or she has got your back—and will be there to help you get back on your feet, should you stumble and fall. Your mentor will also be around to hear your story, as well as understand your thoughts and emotions.

Reason 3: **Your mentor is ready to give you constructive criticism.**

Not only does your mentor possess the necessary first-hand experience; he or she is also trained to be a mirror that will show you what you are, what you want to be, and what you have become. This person is not afraid to critique your decisions and actions and offer honest and sound advice that will improve your set of moves towards your goal. He or she will show you the areas where you excel and those that need improvement, and prevent you from making unnecessary mistakes that can cost time, energy, and money.

Reason 4: **Your mentor keeps your discipline in check.**

Your journey towards an abundance mindset is not easy, and there's a chance you might make too many stops, fall off the path, or create dangerous shortcuts. With a mentor, you will have somebody to monitor your progress and call you out for going astray.

Reason 5: **Your mentor encourages you to move forward no matter the obstacles.**

Your mentor is your entire cheering squad that will root for your success. He or she will help you rise above the challenges, spread your wings, and fly to great heights.

Many people think that having a mentor is a sign of weakness, inadequacy, and self-doubt. So what? If you think you need support in your quest for an abundance mindset, which leads to wealth and other manifestations of success, then find a mentor by all means! There's absolutely nothing wrong with that.

* * *

Going back to my contact center that the liquidators shut down more than a decade ago, you might not believe it, but the incident was borne of an unpaid Yellow Pages ad worth $3,000. My staff and I overlooked this relatively small debt, which had accumulated interest and snowballed into a serious problem. I got the lawyers involved and had to pay $15,000 in legal costs. I also spent time getting all the company's affairs cleaned up: disorganized financial reports, unpaid taxes, unattended declarations from suppliers and clients and employees, and all other pending affairs.

I would never forget that day. I came home broken and shattered inside out. The scolding of liquidators and the taunting of employees that were directed at me kept reverberating in my head.

I collapsed on the sofa and closed my eyes. A phantasmagoria of events ran in my head. This yanked me back to my childhood when I saved money to buy my dream remote control car. I did get it, thanks to my thriftiness, but the first time I drove it, I accidentally had it topple off a stone. It fell from the road into a pit. I came home crying with the irreversibly crushed car. My dad told me to be careful with things, which only worsened my pain. My mum said, 'It's not a problem that you lost your car. The problem is that it's your only car.' In my horror, I managed to rouse myself from the nightmare.

I turned on the television to distract myself from the ugly mixture of angst, anxiety, regret, fear, and sadness over my loss. The movie being shown was part of the world-famous *Harry Potter* series. I cast aside my every problem and glued my eyes to the TV. During an interval, there was an intro about JK Rowling, a British novelist who authored the series.

'Once, she was so poor that the bellies of her children were on the mercy of government welfare,' the narrator said of JK Rowling. 'She lived from hand to mouth but kept working on her first novel, *Harry Potter and the Philosopher's Stone.* Compared to then, she is now worth billions.'

I was rapt to hear this. A sudden motivation sparked my mind. I recalled the story about Martha Stewart that one of my teachers told the class. Martha Stewart was an American celebrity who was famous for her homemaking and lifestyle shows and books. Her stamp of approval on products and services was worth billions. She seemed to lead a decent life, until she got involved in securities fraud when she sold her stock in a biopharmaceutical company. Found guilty of a string of felony charges, Martha Stewart was sentenced to five months in federal prison. She was fined $195,000 and ordered to step down from her own company. The setbacks didn't stop the so-called homemaking and lifestyle goddess. Instead of giving up the brand she'd built for decades, she staged a well-publicized comeback after doing time in the correctional facility. She returned with the same passion, continued to evolve, and made millions of dollars more.

Martha Stewart's story was my epiphany. I decided not to give up on my dream as I was left with nothing to lose. So in the wake of my legal issue, I applied the invaluable things I'd learned in my business study and the little experience I had in hand. I sipped coffee and created a business map with actionable ideas that inspired me to plunge into the game again. It was like an adrenaline injection that penetrated my body and made my heart throb.

There was a barrage of questions in my head: How do I boost my business? Should I start a side business to support my existing business? How do I recover from the costs of liquidation and stay out of debt? How does a one-person team face the brunt of upcoming events? More importantly, how will I overcome my feeling of lack and triumph over my fear of having nothing?

And then I met my mentor, Paul. That's when I turned my scarcity mindset into an abundant one that, in turn, allowed me to absorb all the positivity I needed to attract more positivity. This was the point where I subscribed to the so-called LOA philosophy. I started appreciating Ralph Waldo Trine, who at the turn of the twentieth century wrote, 'The law of attraction works universally on every plane of action, and we attract whatever we desire or expect.' I also revered the early-1900s quote of Charles F Haanel: 'The law of attraction will certainly and unerringly bring you the conditions, environment, and experiences in life, corresponding with your habitual, characteristic, predominant mental attitude.'

As for the science of creating the kind of wealth I desired, these were the simple but effective building blocks that Paul taught me to use:

Building Block 1: **Put your body, mind, heart, and soul to getting rich.**

Building Block 2: **See what it takes to gain the riches you want.**

Building Block 3: **Beef up your resources.**

Building Block 4: **Transact with people who will help you attain your objectives.**

Building Block 5: **Devise a back-up strategy.**

Building Block 6: **Reinvest your earnings.**

I thus prepared myself physically, mentally, emotionally, and spiritually to solve my money problems and—as I had wished since childhood—to get rich. I wanted prosperity for myself, my company, and the people who depended on my business. I then did some calculations to determine the exact amount of money needed to fix the liquidation mess, break even, and make a profit. On a clean sheet of paper, I drew a square and divided it into four sections with a cross. I filled up the appropriate quadrants with the strengths, weaknesses, opportunities, and threats pertaining to my situation.

My SWOT analysis gave an incredibly accurate picture of what I did and didn't have, and what I should do and could gain. It served as my basis for setting short-term plans and showed that I must keep an eye on pricing and promotions to stay in the market. The clock was hitting midnight, but I braved calling my human resources staff to get an exhaustive list of the market. A sleepy voice answered at the second ring, and a little wait for my HR person was worth the effort.

With two building blocks laid down, I worked on getting enough funding to get rid of the sword of debts hanging over me. I drew up a list, titled 'Potential Clients', consisting of all the rich and trustworthy existing and prospective customers I'd encountered. I spent the next few days marketing to them.

This part reminded me of that period in my life when I was selling alarms and security systems, although my present action wasn't about calling people from my bedroom. It was about knocking on every potential clients' door in hopes of closing deals and generating the income needed to keep my company afloat. The toil was worth it; I was finally able to get clients. Truth be told, the business that these clients signed on to would not suffice to grow the company. I was grateful, however, that it would yank me out of the liquidators' grip within a month. I was on the road to recovery, but not before learning these lessons: Clear all debts before they're due. Keep the company's records in good shape to avoid any sudden disaster.

Soon after, I made a name in the market with a brand that resonated with clients. I did this following Paul's advice, 'Take the time to understand your customers and consider how they react to what you're saying.'

With my legal and financial obligations fulfilled, I founded a telecommunications company. Going by the saying, 'A wise person can never be bitten by the same snake twice,' I did thorough research on the business first. I made short and long-term plans and planned a backup strategy. I also went to rethink the way I managed people—something I took for granted then—and channeled a good part of the company's resources on building a strong team. I learned along the way that quality employees were the face and strength of the business.

The next and most crucial step was to focus on accounts and operations. This quote by Chuck McLane, lead managing director at the American accounting firm CBIZ, caught my attention: 'Accounting is important when you're starting a business. You've got to know what you're getting yourself into, and numbers can help you figure out if it will be overwhelming, if you can handle it, if you need help.' This was on point.

When you knew the ins and outs of your cash flow, you'd be able to control repayments, debt that came due, deductions for fixed income, payroll, sales tax, and other obligations. Having learned the hard way from the previous havoc, I didn't want to take any more accounting risk.

The telco was a huge success and eventually sold for eight figures. This set a chain reaction of successes in motion.

In the jungle, where the strongest survive and savages rule with no mercy for the laggers, the first step is to be brave. You have to conquer your fear to conquer the jungle. The same holds true for life, where the world is a jungle. Your level of fear decides whether you're a hunter or the hunted. In my case, I was the prey but not anymore. It's time to be a predator, having vanquished my fear with my share of struggles and traumas. After the success of my telco, my confidence was in seventh heaven.

It was the season of bone-freezing winters when I sat in a coffee shop outside my office building. A delivery boy entered the shop. Although dressed in heavy clothes, he was shivering because of the cold. He retrieved an envelope from his pocket and handed it over to the owner. The owner scrutinized the envelope, went to his office, and came out with some cash in his hand. He gave the money to the delivery boy, signed a document, and wished him a good day. There was the basic principle of business in that scene: The delivery boy gave the shop owner what he needed and got compensated in return. As I reflected on this over my cuppa, another business idea hit my mind.

I was good in my field, which made me a go-to person in my area of expertise. This being the case, I decided to start a consultancy. I would partner with three people. We diversified our services to cover a large area of the market. We worked as a third-party contractor, consulting individuals and organizations consultancies on matters of audit, tax, management. We also provided legal, risk, and financial advice. By dint of hard work, my partners and I established a foothold in the market and gained a solid reputation in no time. We then spread our wings and transcended borders. From my end, I set up companies in Australia and the Philippines to cater to clients in the United Kingdom and the United States. I made sure the math was perfect this time—having gone through entrepreneurship hell and back. But, lo and behold! The devil of misfortune hit me hard. Again. It was more devastating this time, though.

Our company's annual session was where we checked our annual progress and decided on the distribution of shares. Our stakeholders, including potential clients, were there to witness the meeting. Everything was going well until it was announced that I only held less than ten per cent of shares whilst my partners had thrice as much. I was shocked. My partners cheated me and stole my rights to the company that I'd created. I was hurt and angry, not only because of the cheating but also because my very own brainchild had gone into someone else's hands against my will. Regardless, I didn't let this break and shatter me. Instead of letting this drama destroy me, I reminded myself that I shouldn't fall prey to panic, anxiety, and the wicked ways of others.

After three years of struggling for the company, I separated myself from my partners and started my own consultancy. Within no time, I made a name in the market again. I still had the scar from the past that reminded me never to ignore the gravity of misfortune. I found comfort in American author Robert Kiyosaki's words, 'A winning strategy must include losing.'

I went on to invest in other things that would generate sources of passive income and found the best place to put some money in: real estate. On weekends and after office hours, I gathered data about property rates, commercial areas, tenants, student property, flipping property, single let, and a host of related topics. I didn't want to leave any stone unturned. Afterwards, I invested in a small to-let area and a series of viable small and large properties. The venture thrived along with my main business, although managing operations single-handedly was no child's play. With hard and smart work, however, I built a strong portfolio of properties. However, I refused to let this real estate success get into my head and exercised caution instead. I anticipated a checkpoint waving at me once I'd achieved something.

Human life was like a juggling act where people should keep many objects balanced. If one of the objects failed, my whole show would be ruined. This was starting to happen to me. Everything seemed to be on track. My company was running smoothly. The numbers were in good condition. But the workload and routine were too disturbed and disturbing. I had to do frequent meetings and tours to sustain the company's image. My life was a pendulum between work and family, and I had very little time for myself. I was alone with many unbalanced things on my plate, and something was missing. Satisfaction.

I remembered Paul and his teachings. I'd owned the abundance mindset, thanks to his perseverance, but somewhere along the way, I set it aside. I missed out on the fact that I should wear it at all times. If I chose the path of success, it should be success with satisfaction. No compromises.

Recently, I got involved in network marketing. The money making and the wealth building system seemed absurd at first, but I soon felt its potential. The environment was free. The market was global, and every participant could have any client from anywhere in the world. There was no need for face-to-face transactions. All the essential tools, such as directory

Websites and social media platforms, were available online. I took advantage of the work freedom that this venture offered and combined it with my inborn diligence and industriousness. Long story short, I made good money from it. Moreover, I felt satisfaction.

My network marketing experience affirmed my 180-degree turn. I was no longer lacking and wanting in any aspect of life. I spent more time engaging in activities that made me absorb as much positive energy as I could. I mulled over the tug-of-war between becoming successful and unsuccessful—my forwards and backwards, my ups and downs, as a successful struggler. I appreciated every lesson in my transformation from loser to winner, and I was grateful for everyone and everything that helped me gain my life's victory.

One day soon, I'll share my story and insights with other people in pay-it-forward fashion—that is, if they want to get rich in material things as they find abundance in mind, heart, and spirit.

"THE KEY TO ABUNDANCE IS MEETING LIMITED CIRCUMSTANCES WITH UNLIMITED THOUGHT."

~Marianne Williamson

CHAPTER FOUR

From Death to Divine
Shifting the Perception of Abundance

By Harmony Polo

In 2003, my life took a radical shift from a seemingly abundant and prosperous life to a humble one, living as a global nomad in pursuit of answers. I went from the glitz and glitter of a Hollywood A-lister's life to living in a studio villa in Bali, Indonesia. After a nine-year-long sabbatical, I found the answers I was looking for and returned to live in America to share my new defined relationship to abundant living.

My illusionary successful life as a high-profile hairstylist to Hollywood stars was filled with abundance, wealth, fame, and material belongings in a picture-perfect world. I had the financial means to do everything I desired, living life flying around in private jets, receiving personal invitations to A-list celebrities' homes, and dripping in designer clothes, fashionista handbags, and the bling of bling's. One would think having all of this would automatically equate to happiness, joy, and love. However, my experience taught me quite the contrary. Always being "camera-ready", I looked happy, confident, and emanated success, which was the visual envy of many. However, inside, I was angry and numb; I had actually created this numbness in an attempt to escape internal turmoil, until the day circumstances drove me to the hospital where I had my first near-death experience.

With every epic turning point in life, experiences are created to teach us what we need to learn in this lifetime, and sometimes, these teachings are hard and painful. My journey began in 1993, when on the eve of my seventeenth birthday, my father passed away. I had no foundational education on how to process profound loss, which birthed confusion and anger. Consequently, many decisions I made during this time were not necessarily the healthiest choices as they were created out of anger and riddled with sabotage, selfishness, and isolation. My anger was a murky dark cloud that manifested many grim realities, which in retrospect, supported my reasoning to embrace my atheist beliefs. Living as a committed atheist, I no longer wanted or was interested in a connection with God and held a laser-beamed focus to avoid any topics associated with God; with my dark and angry judgements, I regarded people who talked about God as stereotypical hypocrites. The judgements and bitterness swallowed my heart like an armored shield, ready to provide protection until the day life gave me no other choice but to surrender.

Stretched out on a cold gurney, the smell of the sterile hospital overwhelmed my nervous system as the lights above created a terrifying internal roller coaster that filled me with fear and anxiety. I wondered why this was happening to me as I felt alone, isolated, and scared. What was happening to the invincible rock-star hairstylist? As I was being admitted to the hospital, the unsettling feelings were like the sound of nails scratching a chalkboard. However, as dreadful as it was, that experience at the hospital, in 2009, ultimately ended up being the most significant wake-up call that initiated my awakening journey.

After six days of intense pain, drugged with the strongest narcotics, and with an anti-biotic IV drip stuck in my arm, I was still showing no signs of improvement. At that point, the doctors wanted to cut my neck open to remove the resistant MRSA staph infection, but with every cell in my body shuttering, I firmly said "NO" to the procedure. That very night, my atheist body hobbled to the bathroom and shut the door so that nobody could see my fragile heart fall apart. As I looked deeply into the mirror, my eyes became portals to my soul as my invincible and powerful ego uttered the words, "if there is a GOD, you will reveal yourself, here and now, and take this infection out of my body. By doing so, I will commit my life to you." With tears flowing uncontrollably from my eyes, I crawled back into bed. The tears wet my pillow as I drifted into a deep sleep. When I woke up the next day, I felt different; something had happened, but I could not identify what it was. I felt life pulsing through my veins and a degree of clarity I had never felt before.

As I swung my legs over the edge of the bed to prepare myself to stand, I kept hearing my prayer over and over in my mind, like a record skipping to repeat the same verse. As I made my way to the bathroom to start my morning routine, I grabbed my toothbrush to start brushing my pearly whites, turned on the water, and looked at the mirror to discover that the infection was completely gone. I pinched my arm, squinted my eyes in disbelief, and realized that my prayer had been heard! Questions were flowing through my mind: "Did this really happen? Am I dead? What will happen now?" All I knew was that it was real; I made a deal with the big chief, and now, step one would be recovery. After being discharged from the hospital, my prayer and commitment sang sweet symphonies in my ears, reminding me of my words and choices. I had many hurdles to cross, such as detoxing from all the narcotics and strengthening my weakened body. At this point, the real work had to begin. This was the beginning of a long and arduous road, which opened my reality and redefined my relationship to abundant living.

As soon as my immune system was as strong as a racehorse's, in 2010, I booked my ticket to Bali to meet this person called the Medicine Man. To me, this was the furthest thing away from what I considered to be "normal"; however, I felt that there was some mystical reason why I needed to meet him. My burning commitment to understanding what a Medicine Man was ended up being the pinnacle of my nine-year sabbatical. I never intended to live in Bali; I planned to visit for only three weeks, leaving as a changed person. Little did I know that this magical place would become my home for the next nine wonderful, yet most challenging, years of my life. I wonder where the handbook was with the directions to this journey; why didn't I see the neon sign flashing in front of my eyes that said, "this journey you are about to embark on will require the most challenging work, yet will come with the highest rewards"? Where is the finish line? When would the job be complete? Blind faith became my guide.

As the airplane doors opened, the soft waft of Bali was like medicinal love. It was familiar, yet so foreign. From the moment my feet touched the land, it was like a loving magnetic pull that felt familiar. I felt safe. I felt free. This was the day my greatest teacher, Bali, welcomed me to discover who I am and how to love myself, which redefined my meaning to abundance. I went from wearing posh *Manolo Blahnik* and *Jimmy Choo* shoes to happily having my feet bare on the earth. My body cells felt alive and were vibrating in a whole new way. I felt activated and craved for more as I ditched my rose-colored glasses and welcomed curiosity as my teacher in this majestic university of life.

As the massive successful life I created in Hollywood crumbled, the birth of a new reality gracefully revealed itself as

Bali welcomed me with open arms, frangipani blessings, bells ringing, temples chanting, and, of course, every single skeleton in my closet that I thought I had escaped from. How could I be in the most beautiful place on earth and feel as low and depressed as I did? My mind was successfully activated. Going from a workaholic schedule to no schedule at all, I had plenty of time on my hands to write some great stories to enhance my Oscar winning drama movie. As Facebook ripped my ego to shreds, I watched my colleagues celebrate working with "my" clientele, flying around the world, and eating fancy dinners. Watching this on Facebook was like being served a serious slice of humble pie and not being invited to a private home or a fancy dinner to enjoy it.

During the first year I lived in Bali, I would fly back and forth to the U.S. to take care of private clients and weddings. This small tether to my work felt like holding onto something that was slowing dying off. After one of my long trips to the U.S., I arrived back in Bali jet lagged and confused. I did not know whether I should scratch my watch or wind my head. I had decisions to make about my upcoming trip to India, yet something continually prevented me from making these decisions. I felt a deep calling to India, like a spiritual intervention, yet I could not identify what and where this would take me until my ravenous jet-lagged hunger was satiated. Sitting in a quaint Bali cafe, the smell of organic vegetarian food calmed my rumbling hunger as I sipped on a perfectly warmed Ojas tea. My jet lag felt like an aerobic workout for my eyelids as I steadily held them open.

Finally, the moment I had been waiting for appeared in front of my eyes like a bright white light, as a burst of energy zapped me awake like the sun. I felt warm, excited, and curious. As I patiently waited for the right moment to speak to this beautiful woman who emanated love and joy from every cell of her presence, butterflies fluttered in my stomach and my tongue felt twisted like a perfect pretzel. The words came to me, "what is your secret? Who is your teacher? Where do I need to go to be taught by your teacher?" She answered, "India", and as such, my plans to India were defined. I immediately signed up to study at the same university in an attempt to discover the source of her happiness and joy, and thus, my first trip to India began with only a plane ticket and with no concrete plans other than my new path toward spiritual studies.

Wheels down. It is 2010, and my feet are now on the motherland of India. The total chaos, sea of infinite people, horns blazing, and extreme heat were overwhelming. I had seen India in movies but had never realized what it would be like in the flesh. As I walked out of the airport into the crowd of people with signs excitedly screaming the names of their guests, I found my driver and name on a poster board and sighed in relief as I was escorted to the car by a lovely gentleman. He drove me through the extremely hectic traffic lanes to an oasis-a surreal paradise hotel. How could such a beautiful place exist amongst such chaos?

Welcome to India.

As I woke up the following morning in this fairytale-like hotel, I ate a five-star meal to prepare for the long and bumpy travel to the university, which was an education in itself. What happened to the pristine paved roads, proper signs, streetlights, and driving on the right side of the road? As I was thrown around in the back seat of the car, I gasped for air, pearls of sweat rolling down my forehead, as the terror of driving gave me heart palpitations. I was neither in control of my safety, nor could I communicate my words with the vast language barrier. I was in the eye of my internal storm - the storm of surrender. With every great storm comes great liberation because this drive of terror ended up changing the course of my life forever. Since then, this metaphor has continually graced me with unimaginable gifts.

Thus, in 2010, my deep spiritual journey began. The whole experience was beyond anything I could imagine or expect. How could I? I never even once thought something like this even existed. I believed that life was just what I had known until that point and that nothing much could happen. I cried many rivers and begged for change. I even considered ending my life. Boy, am I happy that I did not! This was the time of flip-phones, sim cards, and even dial-up internet in some areas. That time was actually a blessing in so many ways, as the earthly and modern distractions we currently face were absent, thereby allowing me to turn the outside world off, and focus on why I traversed such great lengths to southern India's dry and rural lands.

On the first day, the radiantly beautiful monks, dressed all in white, met with our group to discuss the rules and guidelines of living on campus, as we would be living in close quarters, observing *Mauna* (silence), eating meals together, observing strict guidelines between the male and female dormitories, and whatever else was presented to us. Even though they spoke of "the process" we would be going through, everything was still a mystery and strangely exciting. The cardinal rule was that all phones must be off during "the process". As a good student seeking praise from the monks and perfect grades, I listened carefully and observed closely. Every day as I walked up to the main halls, I turned off my phone like an obedient prized student and placed it safely in my tote bag, until one day, the joke was on me. On that day, the plan was to focus for a whole 15 hours on the "parent process". *Gulp*. All the pain and anger I had been holding onto since my father's death in 1993 erupted with a phone call. How was this possible when I was sure I turned off my phone? I was a prized student who listened correctly and was obedient, and yet, my phone magically rang as all the participants in the room started going into a manic hysteria during the first part of the "parent process". I felt like I was in an asylum going mad. As I rustled to find my phone, a mysterious voice spoke to me, and like a flip of a switch, the very first *maha* (grand) awakening began to unravel.

For the next three days, as I wept tears of pain, I saw what I created; I saw my part in the whole situation; it was like being in an Oscar-winning drama movie that I produced, featured, and starred in. It was the awakening that launched my passionate quest for more truth as I discovered all the lies which I had told myself for pretty much my whole life until then. The whole experience was full of uncontrollable tears, laughter, and mania, and from that point forward, the quest for truth became my life-long passion. This experience was only the beginning, and it will never end, which is why I am extremely excited about it. This experience opened my eyes, deepened my relationship with my mother, and gave me the most powerful teachings, such as "things" do not identify who I am. It taught me how to find a deeper connection and balance between work, relationships, self-care, and so much more. It showed me that abundant living occurs when a balance has been restored in all relationships, especially the relationship with oneself. As I have grown in my relationship with myself and all aspects of giving, I can feel that I have created an abundant existence because now that my cup is full, I have so much to give.

After spending nine wonderfully amazing, yet painful, years living in south-east Asia, the balance has been restored in my heart as I have learned to listen to my inner spirit. I understand now that when I choose not to listen, the universal spanking is hard, painful, and intense. My internal relationship with my spirit is a continual practice, and it will never end. It is the greatest relationship I have ever been in, and like every relationship, it takes work and dedication. As I deepened my relationship with my inner spirit, I have learned to trust my inner voice. I have done some crazy things to build this relationship, such as fasting for 40 days to deepen my relationship with the Divine Mother, crawling into caves in India, bathing daily in the Ganga river, learning to sing *Mantra* in Sanskrit and other languages, and so on.

On one of the most beautiful sunny mornings in Bali in 2019, my internal voice spoke to me and said, "It is time to go home", and I knew the time had come for me to return to my native land to share the gifts bestowed upon me in the past nine years. I immediately took action to sell all my belongings, as another layer of letting go taught me a greater depth of surrender. With no defined place to live, carrying my heavy luggage and musical instruments, I boarded the long flight to L.A. As the wheels touched down in Los Angeles, memories flooded my heart. I did not exactly know where I would start this new adventure other than to start with trust. Before landing, I scheduled a short tour in Chicago at the Flowering Heart Center to present a *Sat Sang* and *Kirtan* to teach about commitment: "The level in which you commit is the level in which you're ready to receive". Little did I know at that time that, on this miraculous night, my future husband would be one of the participants.

As such, I was welcomed back into the United States embraced with so much love. As I continually explore the next chapter of my spiritual journey, which is the balance of family, friends, business, community, and love, it is time to integrate my vast spiritual life with my passion for business to create a newly defined relationship with abundant living. I am continually amazed by the power of the universe and the laws of manifestation as I deepen my relationship with awareness, power of words, success, integrity, creativity, passion, sensitivity, empathy, and compassion. Creating my abundant life has evolved in so many ways, from once being defined by material belongings to a balanced life between self-care, family, relationships, friendships, nature, and animals. I understand that success will present itself to me in a very new way, including opening a Harmonic Egg healing center in Naperville, where I happily reside, and evolving my musical journey with Mantra, Spiritual and Business Coaching, and Sacred Haircuts. It has been an absolute joy to merge my spiritual studies with my businesses to develop this newly defined relationship to abundant living.

"ABUNDANT LIVING MEANS ABUNDANT GIVING."

~ E. Stanley Jones

CHAPTER FIVE

A Guide to the New Normal

By Anastasia Gunawan

A small glimpse of sunrise and whispers of dry cold air make their way through my window curtains. As my five senses slowly awaken from a deep sleep, I feel the surface of soft sheets on my skin. My eyes swivel around for a quick sight. I can barely lift my eyelids. I am in a state of hypnagogic, a lucid state between dream and conscious world. I stretch my hands, legs, and torso to awaken my body, like a caffeine jolt to a sleepy brain. I awaken to a very familiar morning routine with an insatiable appetite for a cup of hot, roasted, specialty coffee.

I enjoy a ritualistic approach to making a cup of coffee. I love the pour over or drip coffee method. I slowly dispense coffee beans into my coffee grinder, set to a carefully calibrated measurement for the freshest and best flavor extractions for the cup. As the coffee completes its transformation from whole beans to ground, the aroma of the roasted coffee beans starts to linger in the kitchen. I recognize the scent of cherry fruits with subtle undertones of sweet caramel as my olfactory system continues to savor it a minute longer. I reach for my Chemex (a non-porous glass shaped like an Erlenmeyer flask), a cone filter, and a scale to prepare for brewing. My morning magic drip begins by adding 200^0 F water on freshly-ground coffee methodically set at the cone filter's bottom. Every feeling from this ritual is grounded in the present, a commodity for an abundant life.

**"Realize deeply that the present moment
is all you will ever have."**
~ Eckhart Tolle

It's easier than ever to get trapped in an unconsciously fast-paced life. A study done by Marks & Spencer estimates that roughly nine out of ten people are living life on autopilot.[1]. I hear the same from close friends or family: "I can't seem to get out of this rut," "I feel stuck in life," or "My life sucks!" Many of the patterns I've witnessed from such grievances come from living life on autopilot. Deliberate practice of awareness, reflection and gratitude are indispensable for an abundant life! We are not meant to live on autopilot. In neuroscience, an intentional way of awareness, reflection, and gratitude reinforces neural linkages that set a tone for mind and body throughout our daily lives.

It's challenging to have the presence of abundance without a practice of deliberate creation of abundance. Creating abundance requires a mindset to be completely entranced with the present moment. Indulging in a tasty cup of beverage is a conscious daily creation of abundance. My sense of taste and smell (thank you, olfactory system!) is a powerful catalyst to infinite experiences that enrich and enliven my conscious experience. I deliberately create an experience of awareness, in that present moment, of how the coffee smells and tastes, with gratitude for my healthy body, which is experiencing this simple daily act. And I know that the next several decisions that

---

[1] Autopilot Britain (2017) https://corporate.marksandspencer.com/documents/reports-results-and-publications/autopilot-britain-whitepaper.pdf

need my attention will come from this place of awareness, reflection, and gratitude. I call this deliberate practice priming, also often referred to as mental or physical grounding.

On a normal week, Tuesday can feel like standing in quicksand. The clock is ticking, a perfectly curated to-do list to complete, meetings to attend, reaching out to at least one friend a day, going to the gym – and all this while holding myself accountable to self-care as a priority. Once I was driving down a narrow path in my neighborhood late Tuesday afternoon. A mental picture of my to-do list started to flash into my awareness. I caught myself drifting from the present moment with both of my hands on the wheel. I paused my thoughts for a moment. In this empty space, I recalled my physical grounding from earlier that day. Only from this open space, I had the opportunity to consciously redirect my attention to the magnificent view through my car's windshield. I noticed the trees were breathing with the wind. Living in a high desert in the middle of the fall season, I witnessed trillions of leaves turn into a masterpiece filled with red, brown and yellow, orange hues painted against a backdrop of baby blue sky.

~ Abundant Living Code #1: Prime your mind and body at least once a day ~

Examples of other priming exercises:

- Preparing a fresh, wholesome meal
- Incorporating scent (essential oils) to ground the mind and body
- Dancing and shaking like no one is watching to a favorite song
- Slow breathing, beginning with five inhales and five exhales.
- Journaling with intention
- Nature watching

- Taking a cold shower
- Practicing Yoga

Nature is one of the bountiful gifts of the universe that supply an infinite experience of abundance. Nature always takes me to a place of awe and wonder. I've learned from nature, watching how powerful human perception and imagination create a version of abundant living. Imagination is one of the greatest faculties that man has been given. Even a physically blind person can access the world of imagination. On days that I find it hard to see abundance in the moment, I consciously create it through exercising my personal imagination and journaling.

There are many ways to approach journaling. Every journaling method has a specific intention and purpose. I use journaling as another priming technique to create neural pathways and a blueprint for my version of abundant living. I journal to create a feeling. As Rhonda Byrne, the author of *The Secret*, suggested, "Feeling is The Secret."

Here is one of my excerpts exercising personal imagination and journaling from April 28, 2020:

- I dream of a time where laughter, celebration and bliss can be attained anywhere in the world.
- I dream of a clear ocean with sea creatures, white sand, warm sun rays touching my skin playfully.
- I dream of a place where my heart is whole, and my mind is heaven.
- I dream of fresh, delicious breakfast and dinners in paradise.
- I dream of being free with no care in the world.
- I dream of a time where we can all dance under the moonlight with our bare feet against a backdrop of fire and stars radiating the dark sky like a diamond.

- I dream of abundance, social connection with others, and infinite love for one another.
- I dream of spectacular nights under the aurora on ocean side beach.
- I dream of being wild, one with nature.

Dreams are imaginative play in sleep and waking life. The famous speech, *I Have a Dream*, by Martin Luther King (MLK) is a powerful imaginative play manifested in the art of rhetoric language. MLK was and remains an influential figure of African American history for orchestrating an unprecedented civil rights movement in the 20th century. His speech employed a specific rhetoric element of pathos (a quality that evokes emotions). MLK made an emotional appeal of empathy when he described how slave owners treated African Americans for centuries as living in a "lonely island of poverty" and described the reality of racism to nature like a "dark and desolate valley." *I Have a Dream* speech progressively developed into a plan, using pathos, for living in the USA with flames of ambition free from racism and chains of inequality using repetitive symbolism. MLK inspired millions in his intended audience, yet I find his speech and technique so inspirational in building the blocks of abundant living for each of us. Much of what he created in his speech are emotions and feelings beyond scripted black ink on folded white papers.

I imagine being on the steps of Lincoln Memorial, Washington D.C., witnessing history with the crowds on the day MLK delivered his speech. His letters coming alive, with every text peeling off crimped cappuccino-white papers and dancing in the crowds. The letters invoke a diverse range of emotions, like the colors that make up the rainbow. Though these words were spoken in 1963, MLK still inspires many generations to live an abundant life.

~ Abundant Living Code #2: Understanding is the language for the mind, but Feeling is the language for the body. ~

Creating a feeling of abundance through priming has many advantages. First, the body has a natural gut response to external stimuli before the brain starts to process or become aware of what is happening. Dream journaling re-programs and strengthens this natural response for the body. Dreaming can be a powerful door to the path of every experience you want from life. It is the secret ingredient to unleashing and manifesting an abundant life. One dynamic, life-changing prompt I use for my abundance blueprint is the following question.

When you think of wanting money, what do you honestly and authentically want to get with it?

Here's the list I wrote on my blank sheet of paper:

1. Perfect Health
2. Freedom
3. Ability to give and share with others
4. Adventure, travel, and meeting friends across continents
5. Community

Did you notice the prompt had the words "wanting money" in it? Once you have completed your list, we are going to turn this into an abundance affirmation code. Sustainable materialism is a by-product of abundant life. Many in North America practice the opposite. We sacrifice many days of our lives outside of our abundance code to earn money that will eventually buy us the abundance we seek in our lives. There's a secret to accessing the abundance code. It's a simple, factual concept: a body on autopilot cannot notice or feel the gentle abundance knocking in daylight or night. Abundance is omnipotent and inclusive. It's a fascinating insight about both the eye and the guts – channels of non-verbal human communication – that reveals a lot about possibilities of creating an abundant life.

~ Abundant Living Code #3: Notice what makes your eyes and gut light up. ~

Perception of abundance is like a trickster. Leonardo da Vinci used a keen understanding of perception to blend his famous Mona Lisa smile using neuroscience and optical science. From one angle, Mona Lisa has a demure expression. When you look at her from a different angle, the Mona Lisa smile is cheerful. Her smile is not a mystery anymore, rather an excavation of the science behind the human perception. Da Vinci realized that light rays do not come to a single point in the human eye but instead hit the whole area of the retina. I urge you to become the Da Vinci of your masterpiece. Living abundantly requires a very pragmatic view of our personal abundance code. Once I started to apply this to my own life, I began to file as many experiences as possible that make my eyes and gut lit up (like a thousand crowd saying YES!), or MEGLU.

Here's what my experiences of MEGLU look like:

1. MEGLU when I practice giving and sharing with others.
2. I indulge in adventure and travel because of MEGLU. It puts me on a path to meet others like minded that can assist me with new opportunities.
3. Freedom MEGLU. It is my fuel and energy to attract money.
4. MEGLU when I participate fully in my community using my gifts and talents.
5. Health is my number one priority because health is synonymous with wealth.

The list above is my list of affirmations. I harness the power of MEGLU to supercharge my life to receive the items I wrote in response to the prompt, "When you think of wanting money, what do you honestly and authentically want to get with it?" In addition to receiving your desired outcome, the benefits of living abundantly include being grounded, personal joy, happiness, and connection to mother, earth, life force (chi).

Take 5-10 minutes to draft experiences that make YOUR EYES AND GUT LIGHT UP

~ Abundant Living Code #4: Date and nourish your body with healing foods. ~

Every experience that lights us up through our eyes, and in our gut requires a resonance that must go through the physical body. I experienced a journey of chronic pain, negative resonance, that ultimately brought me to understand that the body is sacred. When I co-authored the *A Journey of Riches Liberating Your Struggle* book, I recounted moments of feeling disease. I neglected my body, feelings, and series of burnout episodes because I wasn't aware of the paradigm of scarcity and low self-worth accompanied by the trauma I had experienced as a child. At that time, I desperately wanted to heal my body. During this early journey of personal healing, and designing real abundance, I committed a period to learn the natural rhythm and flow of my physical body.

During this journey of healing my physical body, one of my coaches introduced me to Human Design. Human Design is a system introduced by Alan Krakower in 1922. In Human Design, aspects of eastern astrology (I-Ching & Chakras) and Jewish mysticism (Kabbalah) are combined to explain how each individual is built to respond to the world from the Body-Graph[2]. The BodyGraph is unique to each person and is defined by the time and place of birth. There are four Human Design archetypes. Each archetype response distinctively to the internal and the external worlds with sets of unique characterizations. According to the BodyGraph, I belong in the generator archetype with a defined Root Center (one of the body chakras). Some consequences, among the strengths, of having a defined root center are developing obsessive compulsive behaviors, improperly initiating situations, and natural tendencies to feel insurmountable pressure from within.

Understanding some aspect of myself through the BodyGraph helped me find root causes of the negative events that transpire in my life. The consequences of an individual with an unbalanced, defined Root Center bring about the stress that the individual isn't designed to handle; that can undermine your health. This experience of learning about honoring and learning about my body (reactions, responses, and design) ultimately revealed the secret to living my best life in my design which is following what makes my eyes and gut light up (refer to abundance code #3).

For a generator with a defined Root Center to flourish, the gut is the ultimate decision maker. Cultivating a meaningful language with my gut did not come easily. Exhaustion, stress and disease weaken gut health, and starting from square one, relearning to tune back to my body for wisdom, I surrender completely to the power of healing foods. Cooking became an immense part of my life. The simple act of cooking makes me feel excited, alive and creative. I can choose freely (one of my abundance codes is freedom) what dish I want to prepare, and which of a million ways I can approach that dish. It's never a

---

[2] The Rave BodyGraph. Source: https://www.mybodygraph.com/

dull moment. Do I want my scallions diced or sliced? Do I want to slow roast lamb, or am I feeling adventurous today with my sous vide machine? Even with a day full of stressors and problems at work that constantly need solutions, I find stress relief in the kitchen. Cooking is a therapeutic treatment for individuals with stress, depression, or anxiety. Cooking is a part of my abundance code that was not taught in my early childhood. I started learning cooking and how much I enjoyed it in my adulthood. It is never too late, at any age, to discover new avenues to support your abundance code and commit to them!

Here's a recipe for delicious, healing and abundant food. My gut says YES!

Healing Khichdi

Ingredients

1. 1 cup of white basmati rice
2. ½ cup yellow moong dal
3. 2 tablespoons ghee
4. 1 tablespoon Khichdi spice mix
5. 1 teaspoon Himalayan salt
6. 6 cups of water
7. 2 cups of seasonal vegetables

* Khichdi spice mix (1/2 teaspoon each) consisting of black mustard seeds, cumin seeds, turmeric powder, coriander powder, fennel powder, grated ginger.

Instructions

Soak moong dal overnight. Rinse rice with water at least twice until the water runs clear. In a medium saucepan, warm ghee over medium heat. Add Khichdi spice mix until aromatic. Stir rinsed rice and dal into spices and sauté for a few moments, stirring constantly. Add six cups of water, turn heat to high, and bring to a boil. When the soup comes to a boil, stir in the salt, reduce heat, cover, and simmer for about forty minutes— slice vegetables into small, bite-sized pieces. About halfway through the Khichdi's cooking process, stir in the vegetables and allow the stew to return to a boil. Continue to simmer until the rice, dal, and vegetables are fully cooked. Remove from heat, cool, and serve. Garnish with cilantro, fresh lime, or flax-seed oil.

Khichdi has been referred to as The Food of the Gods. It is said that Khichdi was the favorite food of the Hindu god Go-rakshnanth, a yogi saint and influential founder of the Nath Hindu monastic movement in India. A scientific explanation for the healing powers of Khichdi lies in moong dal. Moong dal is a complete protein food, high in nutrients and antioxi-dants. In Ayurveda, moong dal is a staple for cleansing the mind and the body.

It is both a powerful and abundant act of creation to under-stand, nourish and commit to rituals to honor our bodies. In times like these, our personal commitments to transcend to a level of abundant living will ultimately pave the way to a new world and a new way of living. Martin Luther King embodied his idea of abundance for people through his rhetoric speech. Could you begin to imagine what impact YOU can make by embodying your abundance code every day around your fam-ily and social network?

Allow me to return to that vivid memory of the early morning hours that took place late winter in mid-February 2020, when I held tight to a hot coffee mug and basked in short moments of physical and mental grounding for the day. I closed my eyes briefly while the entire world was shaken, stretched and twisted upside down by pandemic waves no one could escape.

Before entering the world, a battlefield of deaths, disease, and distress, I ripped out a single paper from my notebook and swiftly scribbled:

How to live an Abundant Life Effortlessly during a Global Pandemic:

1. Prime once a day.
2. Feel your emotions, awaken the senses and your body.
3. Prioritize actions that make my eyes and gut lit up.
4. Nourish my body with healing foods.

I was priming for my day as a pandemic/emergency medical first responder, working the front lines serving and protecting my community from COVID. I took the first sips of my drip coffee and knew the months following that morning would never again be the same.

It has been 400 days since that morning. In the midst of uncertainties, global fear and a mental health emergency that transpire from sustained periods of quarantine and social distancing, a deliberate life design transcending a multitude of "dark and desolate valleys", and "lonely island of loneliness" came into fruition.

In retrospect, 2020 presented many challenges. The faces of trauma, loss and death forced many, including myself, to develop a code to continue living life abundantly. Which will you choose today? Here's a glimpse of the life design I affirmed as abundance code in this chapter to help you navigate into a new normal. I urge you to deliberately create, reflect, and commit to your personal abundance code today, and I hope to see you in this new world just on the other side of this magnificent sunrise.

"LIVING THE ABUNDANT LIFE IS DIFFERENT THAN KNOWING ABOUT IT. IT'S TIME TO BEGIN PRACTICING THE LIFE WE WERE MADE FOR."

~ Mark Beeson

CHAPTER SIX

Mastering Opportunities
With Abundant Living

By Samuel Sykes II

There are two ways to venture through life: by living in scarcity, or living in abundance. When we live in scarcity, we worry if there will be enough for us, let alone everyone else. We feel that life is inherently limited and confined, and we can only push up against that limit, not break through it. We artificially restrict ourselves, masking our natural-born talents and damaging our relationships. When we live in scarcity, fear is at the heart of everything we do.

When we live in abundance, we don't worry about limits. We understand that life is what we make of it, and we can decide to make the world a place where there's enough for everyone. We feel that we have so much that's good inside of us, and so we have so much to give. We live lives of exuberant joy and equanimity because we understand that as others gain, whether in wealth, health, or love, we can gain as well. Their success is not our failure, and, thus, we can both share in the joy that comes with living lives of passion. When we live in abundance, love and hope are at the heart of everything we do.

However, living a life of abundance is not easy. It's not as simple as flipping a switch or pressing a button. Sometimes the world conspires against us; it pulls us down into a mindset of scarcity, a mindset of fear. It's easy and tempting to be sucked into that mindset, but well worth it to resist it. Because at the other end of that spectrum is a life of abundance, a life of hope. It's a life that takes work to get to and work to maintain, but every minute of hardship yields a bountiful return, as you find yourself more at peace, more hopeful, more loving, and more successful.

Passion is absolutely critical to living a life of abundance. Your passion is as personal as your fingerprint: it's unique to you, and only you can decide how to pursue it. However, while you can just look at your thumb to see your fingerprint, your passion can be much more elusive. Some are aware of their passion from the moment of their birth, while others can spend years of dedicated effort trying to find it. You have to look inward, considering what it is that truly makes you happy before it will reveal itself to you.

When it does, it can be a truly joyous feeling. However, it can also be scary, full of pressure, expectations, and fear. In *How Much Joy Can You Stand? A Creative Guide to Facing Your Fears and Making Your Dreams Come True,* Suzanne Falter-Barns tells us that, "the truth is that dreams can be both tantalizing and frightening. They call upon us to be our bigger selves, possibly bigger than we've ever been...so we extend our reach out into the world and finally begin to touch our lives as we are meant to."

With great power comes great responsibility, and the same is true of great passion. It can be terrifying to face the reality of caring about something so deeply that we're willing to fully commit ourselves to it; however, it can also be liberating and transformative. Passion is the driver that can make us willing to put everything we have into a project or idea, and risk great amounts to see our dreams fulfilled.

However, passion is just the first part of living a life of abundance. Passion without effort is like a recipe without a chef. The second part is, naturally, hard work, dedication, and effort. Only by working towards your dreams can you bring them any closer to being achieved. Only by throwing yourself wholeheartedly into a mission can you enact change in the world. I was raised in a tight-knit family filled with love and virtue. My parents and grandparents always stressed the profound importance of a strong work ethic. They told me, "If you work hard and do what you need to do, good things will happen."

During the winters of my teenage years, while my friends were all out playing in the snow, I was working for the local farmer, riding my bicycle for miles on slippery roads to earn some pocket-change and work experience. It was exhausting and difficult, and there were times when I wanted to quit and go have fun with my pals. But I didn't, and that was because I had goals. I had things I wanted to do, and places I wanted to get to. And nothing would stop me from seeing them through.

As such, when unique and exciting opportunities appeared, I was eager to make the most of them. After I graduated high school, one such opportunity presented itself to me. I was given the chance to travel to Panama for both business and personal travel. I got the opportunity to be in meetings with various Panamanian government officials and international corporate executives. While I was there, the high-profile military leader and general, Manuel Noriega, was indicted on drug charges, sending the country into turmoil. An otherwise wonderful business trip quickly turned dangerous as Americans and those in opposition to the government began to be stopped, questioned, and even arrested, for vague and meaningless charges.

I was harassed and threatened; I was pulled over a couple of times on trumped-up traffic charges and forced to pay fines or face the possibility of being sent to jail. It was a terrifying time in my life, one that I wasn't sure that I would get out of alive. I was in the heart of unrest and faced a whole range of threats and dangers.

However, the one thing that helped me get through this time was the love and support of the locals. With most of them either silently or vocally opposing the government, I could lean on them during these challenging times. They helped keep me safe and secure as I navigated this terrible situation for weeks, and in doing so, opened up my mind to a whole world of abundance that existed beyond my home.

The love of these people was so pure and powerful that, even as my life was at risk, I couldn't help but appreciate what I was being given. I was in awe of their culture and the way that they all rallied together and took me in. This experience was the spark that made me realize I wanted to learn as much as I could about the international business world and the diverse cultures it spans.

After leaving Panama safe and sound because of these people, I couldn't help but wonder in amazement at the abundance the world presented before me: even amid terrifying political unrest, I was loved and supported by total strangers. I became convinced that even in dark situations life and love still go on. They exist in abundance even when it seems like they should shrink back into the shadows.

I emerged from my experience in Panama with a resolute commitment to success and following my passion. I began building my skills and knowledge to work towards my goals. I progressed from farm work to being a lumberjack and supporting my family construction business. After working there for a few years, I realized that my hunger for international experience was stronger than ever, so I left to travel the world.

I took in every experience I could, absorbing and savoring everything in the quest to expand my knowledge about the world and the diverse cultures and opportunities that exist within it. I began to get a taste of what international business would be like, and the abundance of opportunities and experiences that came with it, and I knew that I wanted more. These experiences propelled me forward into my business career, allowing me to continue to travel around the world, meeting new people and creating new businesses, products, and inventions.

As I was on my personal journey, one person never lost faith in me: my grandmother. She always told me that she wanted to see me make my first million dollars before she died. I lost her nearly seventeen years ago when she was ninety. I still cling to every letter and gift she gave me; they're mementos that inspire me, remind me why I do what I do, motivate me to keep moving forward, no matter what life throws at me.

When she died, I was crushed, but I knew in my heart that she would always be with me. I felt her spirit move with mine as I set out with a renewed vigor to pursue my goals and follow my dreams. I knew I still had so much to learn in the corporate world, so I sought out those who had already become successful to expand my knowledge and build up my resources. I approached everyone I met with an open heart and pledged to treat them with honesty and respect, just as my grandmother would have told me to do.

I approached business the way I had learned to approach life: with a mindset of abundance. I wasn't out to scam people, rip them off, or take their money. I was out to improve the world, learn about other people and cultures, and learn about myself. I was out to follow my passion.

Unfortunately, not everybody shared my same values. There are unethical people in this world who seek to take advantage of the energy, charm, and success of others, for their own personal gain. They seek to hitchhike on the passion of others and try to pass it off as their own.

Over the past twenty-five years and beyond, people have shortchanged and taken from me, leading to hard financial and crushing emotional losses. I've lost friends and business partners to greed and corruption.

I've been fortunate, with the immense amount of business transactions in which I have been involved, to only ever have to deal with a few unlawful con artists. After I confronted and revealed these swindlers lies, along with the help of Federal Agencies and Law Enforcement Partners, they were held accountable and prohibited from conducting future business. However, when I was in Atlanta, Georgia, I met a man from Michigan. He had come to Georgia to conduct business, and I was happy to help him out. Unfortunately, it wasn't until later that I realized his deception, and I understood that he was bogus who only needed a credible local businessman as a cover for his illegal schemes. I was left to deal with his business deception through a corrupted legal system as he, with his greed, vanished, taking capital, time, and energy from myself and from the other investors.

I was devastated, and it was the only time in my career I felt truly blinded by evil. While it took years for my trust and faith to slowly build back up after being torn down so suddenly, I always remembered that, no matter how difficult and terrible a situation may be, you can always learn, and grow, from it. I kept my gaze cast forward into the future, remembering that life is abundant, even when it sometimes seems the complete opposite.

Experiences like these can be tragic and crushing, but every time someone else took advantage of my open spirit, I sat in the ruins of our professional and personal relationship and thought of my grandmother. She would tell me that there are bad and evil people in this world, but that shouldn't blind me to the beauty and virtue that does exist. Only through faith in God and yourself can you move forward.

She inspired me, through all the tough times, to keep my chin up and my mindset focused on abundance. The world is what you make of it, and unfortunately, there are people out there striving to make it a place of deception and greed. But there are also people out there striving to make it a place of hope and love. A place where there is enough for everyone, and joyful opportunity exists around every corner. Only by focusing on the latter can we bring about that world of abundance.

While enduring the pains and challenges of the years, I never stopped believing that we are designed and created for extraordinary achievement. Even when others looked down on me for my perplexed state of affairs, I never gave up and remembered that each challenge taught me important lessons and allowed me to grow. While the journey can be hard and the struggle can weigh you down, never forget that we live in a world of abundance: there is abundant love, gifts, and talents within yourself and others that, no matter what happens to you, can propel you forward.

These obstacles have given me the knowledge and tools to develop and create hundreds of successful projects and companies. I've mentored, invested, operated, and managed companies through good times and bad, always learning and growing. I've overcome countless obstacles that stand in a company's way, adding the experience to a vast mental library that has only grown over the years. I hope to use my knowledge to help others in the future ride a smoother path on the way to achieving their goals and passions.

I've also visited, worked and explored in over fifty countries, giving me a wide range of global knowledge that is integral to the foundation and success of an international company. I've learned so much about other societies and the international business community, and I've learned the need to adapt to others' cultures. Through my travels, I've encountered so many unique individuals, all of whom have wonderful passions. As I've collected these passions, I can't help but stand firm in my conviction that the world is absolutely full to the brim with passionate people who want to make a difference and share their knowledge with others. Passion is bountiful around the world; the key is how to access that passion for good.

I've also personally worked on hundreds of inventions and patents, with several still active in over thirty countries. My path as an inventor has been rewarding as I've acquired the knowledge of how to use your heart, mind, and soul to determine what business and consumers will require in the future. Through years of hard work creating products to improve the lives of customers everywhere, I've learned how to create ideas that stick, and inventions that make a difference. The world of creation and invention is fundamentally one of abundance; after all, think of all the inventions that have yet to be invented! Think of all the wonderful creations that are just waiting for someone to bring them into existence so that they can get to work connecting people and improving their lives.

And while I've received countless awards, both for my corporate work and my role supporting the success of others, I have always stayed humble, ready to grow. Like a wide-eyed kid fresh out of school, I've always known that there is so much more to learn, and I've never let my success and experience blind me to that basic fact. This has kept me eager to approach others with an open heart and attentive ears, as you never know what someone will teach you, no matter their status or age.

This openness has led to experiences I would never have even dreamed of, like becoming an international karate champion! I would never have thought that I could achieve something like that, and only through my attitude of humility and openness could I have begun to pursue it. Someone with a scarcity mindset would say that they're too busy, or that they don't stand a chance. But one with an abundance mindset says, "Let's do it. What's the worst that could happen?"

By remaining humble even in the face of success, you're able to not only continue to grow at a time when others would stagnate, but you can pass on the gift of your knowledge and lessons to others. You can teach others what you've learned through the challenges of the years, allowing them to avoid such challenges on their road to success.

While I've experienced a blessed life filled with success as well as failure and loss, I experienced my most devastating loss just this past year: losing my mother. In the past, I've lost large sums of money. I've lost business partners and friends. And I've lost emotional strength through the wickedness of others. But nothing compares to the loss of the incredible woman who raised me.

After she passed on, I struggled and suffered, seeing the temptation to slip into a world of hurt and pain. But I always remembered my grandmother and how she taught me that with every loss comes the opportunity to grow, to move forward, to learn.

I turned my pain into passion, realizing that two paths stood before me: one of suffering, doubt, fear, and hopelessness, and one of love, hope, peace, beauty, and abundance. Through the words of my grandmother, I was able to go down the second path, learning, growing, channeling my suffering into positive energy, remembering and honoring my mother for the incredible woman she was, and recognizing her role in making me the man I am today.

The loss of my mother was my toughest challenge to date. But, as with all the others, I remained resolute in my belief that faith will see me through. I dug deeper than I have ever had to before. Through this process, I emerged a better person, more confident than ever that we live in a beautiful world, and that life is abundant when you see it that way.

I like to believe that my grandmother would be proud of where I am today. I've achieved the financial success that she always knew was within me, and being out of the ordinary, I've enjoyed the freedom of choice. I've been able to live my life over the years doing what I want and living where I want; I've had the ability to act or change without constraint and to learn what my heart desires. Just as importantly, I have found my passion and purpose. I've spent my entire career building, learning, and growing, yet I recognize that I am like a child when faced with all that one could possibly experience in this world. But that is not a scary or fearful thought; it's a humbling and wondrous one, filled with possibility and abundance.

My grandmother taught me so much, and all I can do is pay it forward and hope that others can hear her message as loudly and clearly as I can. Be secure within yourself, be secure within your finance, and be secure within your life.

You owe it to yourself to follow your dreams. It'll be a challenge, but there is truly nothing like the exhilaration of facing your fears and emerging a champion.

I've never heard of anyone who regretted following their heart.

"THE SECRET TO ABUNDANCE IN LIFE IS TO BEGIN WITH AN ABUNDANT MINDSET AND A CARING HEART."

~ Debasish Mridha

CHAPTER SEVEN

From Tragedy to Treasure

By Lanelle Martin

I now know that abundant living is almost the opposite of what I learned while I was a teenager and young adult. After living a life that most people would admire or dream of, I undoubtedly realize how fooled I was by the hype of abundant living as I understood it in my years of immaturity. I am here to share an advanced kind of abundant living that you would want your children and their children to learn. Understanding this can change your legacy's trajectory and set your future generations' path toward a comfortable way of life just as our ancestors lived. But first, it will require you to reflect on your values, look within, and be honest with yourself. Would you consider a unique perspective on abundant living – as I and many others have? If not for the extraordinary life I have lived, along with the acquired wisdom and experiences of existence, this life lesson– my purpose, would have been unlikely for me to share and to impact the world!

As a young adult, my mission has been to impact the lives of many positively. I have declared this on my Facebook, Instagram, marketing materials, and introductions, and I also repeat it during my presentations and speeches. Bringing joy and positively impacting others came naturally to me. After living through more challenging times, another segment of my life mission emerged.

It is well known that the native people of Hawaii have what is referred to as the "Aloha Spirit." *Aloha* has various meanings. It can be a warm greeting of hello and goodbye. The Aloha Spirit gives a hug rather than a handshake when introduced to someone; it is the essence of love, peace, compassion, and a mutual understanding of respect. *Aloha* is living in harmony with the people and land around you with mercy, sympathy, grace, and kindness. For me, the Aloha Spirit is an undeniable warm and sincere expression of hospitality toward strangers and those you are introduced to as if they belonged to your family. It manifests when adult neighbors and friends are automatically referred to as "Auntie" and "Uncle," both out of respect and because we embrace the loving Aloha Spirit that engulfs our community. My family and I are authentic givers of the Aloha Spirit, and it has become a part of me; it has stayed with me and served me very well in life.

As I got older, I yearned to leave Hawaii and experience more than the paradise where I grew up. When I moved away from Hawaii, at 25 years of age, I was ready to explore a world I had only seen on television. A few times before, which had raised my curiosity, I had temporarily left the islands before moving away. When I attended Bible College for a summer in the tiny town of Cleveland, Tennessee at Bible College, and during a quick visit to Disneyland in Los Angeles, California, several years prior. I was offered a job as a Co-manager with a company opening a store in downtown Seattle, Washington, USA. Before moving to Seattle, I knew nothing about it other than what my friends, native to Seattle, had shared with me the weeks leading up to my departure. They were concerned about my decision to leave Hawaii and how it might affect my happiness. Their thoughts were, why would anyone want to leave Hawaii, "The Islands of Paradise" in its tropical splendor and radiating with love and sunshine? The one thing they warned me of repeatedly was that I was moving away from a dream environment. Away from a warm tropical paradise to a cold, rainy, and gray place that might leave me weary. Depression is rampant in Seattle, Washington, and they were sure to share that with me. They were right, and they were also wrong. I overlooked the cold, rainy, and gray days until my tenth year in Seattle, when I woke up one day and thought, "oh my goodness, it's so cold, gloomy, and gray here!" However, they were also wrong, as, despite this, I have not yet grown tired of Washington.

Washington State grew on me very quickly. A new world beyond what I had grown up around in Hawaii. There were mountains, lakes, skiing, rivers, and deserts, all in the same state! I was in my mid-twenties when I arrived in Washington state, so I wanted to see it all, do it all, and have it all - and that I did! I attended practically every worthy event and did every tourist thing one could do in Washington State. I recall my friends surprised to learn of all the places I had been to and experienced while living in Washington, which they had not visited despite being natives of the area. Many who lived their entire lives in the state had not experienced a fraction of the site-seeing and events that I had within the short time that I was there.

Upon my arrival to Washington State, I landed the job as a Co-manager of a new downtown Seattle store belonging to the Neiman Marcus group. It was the same company I had started to work at just a few months earlier in Hawaii. They saw something in me to convince the Regional Manager of the Washington location to offer me this promoted position. Promotions and offers happened to me often; I know it has always been God's favor over me. The store had a large footprint in this new downtown Seattle mall. It was a fashion-forward clothing store attracting the latest fashions that most in Seattle were too conservative to wear.

On the other hand, I embraced that type of trendsetting, fashion-forward, flashy, body-conscious, ever-changing, and music-inspired clothing. When outfits were worn by *Madonna, Cyndi Lauper, Janet Jackson*, and *Jennifer Lopes* in the popular hit show *In Living Color* showed up on stage, in music videos, and on television, similar outfits were offered for sale in our stores. As a manager, I led the way and set the stage for my employees by being the first to buy the new arrivals, and never hesitated to adorn myself with the clothing, accessories, and all that our store offered, adding my personal touch and flair to it. As managers, we sold these fun fashion trends and took advantage of our company's great discounts. Those great discounts encouraged the employees to buy and wear its products at work and daily/evening wear; thus, we became a walking advertisement of everything the stores had to offer. We wore noticeable and eccentric accessories, thigh-high boots, stockings, shorts, fancy tops, hats, and exaggerated costume jewelry. It was head-turning, fun, and fashionable clothing, whenever we worked and wherever we went! The "looks" we wore were fun, exciting, expressive, explosive, and sometimes quite revealing, but it was hip and fashionable at the time!

Working at *Contempo Casuals* in downtown Seattle opened many doors and led to some of my best friendships of all time. The web of relationships and network of people that I met grew continuously. It was as if I was born and raised as a popular student body president, PLUS the head cheerleader and prom queen from Seattle, except that I was not. My community expanded quickly, and I made many great friendships; as such, the years following led to an exciting life of abundance for me.

During these times, I enjoyed a lavish life and found myself living in the wealthiest old-money Seattle gated community. My life became filled with excess, fun, an accumulation of fancy things, designer shoes, and clothing, without ever imagining it. I was "gifted" the Mercedes I wanted, flew in private jet planes to ski trips, traveled the seas on private yachts, ate out at world-class 5-star restaurants, and attending the popular formal gala events in the city. We attended opening day events throughout the city and on the famous Lake Washington. I was known to have an abundance of outfits and was fortunate to have a new formal gown for every formal event, never wearing my formal attire twice. I was escorted around in limousines to our evening destinations –formal black-tie events and even nightclubbing with my girlfriends. We accepted invitations from Princes, Sheiks, Hollywood stars, professional athletes, and those organizations' owners to their private events. Fine dining and yachting were some of my favorite regular activities. Finding myself alongside famous actors such as Bruce Willis, Demi Moore, Michael Douglas, and Arnold Schwarzenegger on ski trips became familiar. We hosted "By Invitation Only" soirees for the "beautiful" people in the area. I attended private events amongst the world's wealthiest and was treated well by friends, boyfriends, or myself. This increased my level of false happiness. I indulged and lived abundantly by my definition of the phrase during that particular time in my life.

I worked as a manager/general manager at many other businesses, surrounded myself with many friends, and lived what people consider to be an exciting and fruitful life. After getting married, my husband and I continued expanding our social circles, and we eventually settled down once our oldest son was born in 2004. By then, I was already 41 years old! Up to that point, I had spent years living life with my personal needs being on top of my list, in a way that the majority of the world would consider as abundant living!

As a working Mom, I struggled to juggle my young family's needs while serving my clients and maintaining a successful business. Our full-time nanny, who rotated each child on different days so each could spend time building their social skills at a quality Learning Center, was not enough. My parents lived 5000 miles away, and my in-laws were retired, with no regular babysitting plans. They offered to help twice a month: one child, one day, every other week, which was very much appreciated by my husband and me. I often found myself reaching out to my neighbors and my assistant for last-minute favors to meet my family's needs. Although stressful at times, what carried us through was our incredible community of supportive and caring neighbors, friends, and young teens willing to help at a moment's notice. I valued the help of my community and was incredibly grateful for them.

Belonging to a beautiful and supportive community was a treasure that I appreciated. I began to recognize how much more difficult it would be to live further away in a country setting outside of a suburb or a not-so-friendly neighborhood. I had the vision to develop a supportive community for other parents and caregivers who might be experiencing the hardships of fulfilling their family's needs like I was. It was for those who live alone or away from family, those with children, pets, or aging parents and needed help while they are at work and who wanted peace of mind about their loved ones. It occurred to me that who wouldn't appreciate this type of community support? In 2011, I got excited, pursued my passion, and hired a business coach for direction. I acquired a business name, registered with a business management firm to file our legal documents, and hired a web designer to build our website. My dream was finally becoming a reality. Unfortunately, the website developer eventually became too busy to work on my little project; progress fizzled and, as my family needs grew, my attention shifted away.

In 2017, my husband, our family's primary financial provider, father, and husband extraordinaire, collapsed from a massive heart attack while playing racquetball at our local fitness club. That terrible day changed our lives forever. Fortunately, a young man who got CPR (Cardiopulmonary Resuscitation) certified the day before was there to save his life. This young man later said he believes God intervened and put him at the fitness club that morning when my husband collapsed. I know this to be true. The evening before this happened, my father dreamt that my husband "suffered a heart attack to his death." He immediately began to pray and intervened, asking God to spare my husband's life for the sake of our young pre-teen boys and me. Many mini-miracles happened on this horrific day and the following days that we remain in awe. Thank goodness for my Dad's prayers and God's intervention– my husband is alive today. He suffered a stroke while in recovery at the hospital, but something incredible happened: our greater community embraced our family and took immediate action to support our children, who were 11 and 12 at the time; it was humbling. We received an unexpected and immediate out-pouring of love and support from those whose paths we had crossed over the years in our close and more significant com-munities– those whose lives we may have somehow positively impacted over the years. Mini miracles continued with my family's needs continually met.

Neighbors, teammates' parents, friends, co-workers, nation-wide and internationally, and our out-of-town family instanta-neously stepped in without hesitation to help our sons finish the school year and attend all of their sporting obligations. Our loving community embraced our needs and went out of its way to fill them. We received hot meals on our doorstep prac-tically every day for approximately six months after my hus-band came home from the hospital. Our family friends pro-vided a nurturing, comfortable, and safe place for our younger son during the month I spent in the hospital by my husband's side. Elementary school classmates, who remained friends, generously offered to take both of our sons camping at the start of summer while still in the hospital with my husband. Their gestures were surprisingly and incredibly heart-warming. These were not family members; they were not people we knew for our entire lives– these were parents of my son's classmate from kindergarten and elementary school, parents of our son's teammate for elementary-aged basketball and flag football! We had only met them within the last few years and had never really spent time at each other's homes. Suddenly, distant friends, our local Little League community, Facebook friends, neighbors, parents of kids coached by my husband, worldwide IBM colleagues and partners, a Professional Networking Group I had founded 12 years prior, and many others pitched in to help. They began to schedule themselves on a rotating food delivery once we came home from the hospital. They often checked how we were doing and offered our family help during this turbulent time.

Furthermore, they contributed abundantly toward an expensive one-year therapy for my husband's recovery. A teammate's mom generously brought groceries and toiletries to our home when she went shopping for her own family. Our family and community supported us with loving gestures of finances, a place for my children, food, prayers, love, and help with my husband when I had to work.

We felt absolute abundance, gratitude, and humility. No longer were we interested in fancy clothes, exotic vacations, luxury homes, expensive cars, jewels, designer shoes, and other insignificant things. Instead, living abundantly with love, inclusion, support, and care from a community was at the top of our hearts and minds. Through this experience, we understood that belonging to an expanded community of support is critical. Fear of the unknown allowed me to accept the help I was so accustomed to giving. I am from a family of service, beginning from my grandparents and modeled well by my parents, who have poured into their communities their entire lives. We were experiencing in our time of need the withdrawals from the "Bank of Providence": the financial, physical, and emotional returns from the years of deposits from our parents, ourselves, and our ancestors who generously invested in the lives of others.

For those who have not heard of the term, "The Bank of Providence," I will begin with a few meanings for the word "providence," as found in Google, that resonates with me: A manifestation of divine care or direction; an instance of divine intervention [from 16th c.]; The care, guardianship, and control exercised by a deity; divine guidance. "The Bank of Providence" is a financial institution under the supervision, direction, and management of a divine deity – I translate this deity as God. He multiplies deposits, and the withdrawals manifest that according to the pledges made into such bank. As such, thanks to our investments, we were being blessed with the returns of those deposits made into the lives of others, which turned out to be priceless treasures given to us when we were in the most critical need of it.

My belief in abundant living is now to love, be loved, have self-love, serve others, serve God, and belong to a community that supports you in a way that allows you to live life abundantly. Further, abundant living is to be treasured, give treasures, and cherish people in a way that entices you to serve others every day and in any way possible while remembering to honor yourself and your loved ones while doing so. Every person can benefit from belonging to a support community. My community support network did not happen by accident. It developed over time, and it happened because of the love and support we poured out onto others throughout our lives. It happened through generosity, servant living, and years of watching our parents and their parents serve their communities. It happened because of the relationships we built over time based on trust and camaraderie. It happened by being vulnerable, genuine, and authentic people who genuinely care about others. It happened because we experienced love, gave love, and accepted the love from our community when we needed it.

Embrace your community and invite people into your life purposefully and unreluctantly. Teach your loved ones the skills required to create a giving community around them. Many of our blessings resulted from acquaintances, which developed into relationships and became friendships built through trust. All those who stepped up to help were from our network of friends, colleagues, neighbors, and the greater community. Our parents, grandparents, great grand-parents, and ancestors all belonged to and participated in giving communities. When people can give generously, they will rise to the occasion for those who they witnessed have poured into their communities from their hearts. Communities can change your life forever. It did for our family, and it can work for your family too. Imagine going through life's struggles without access to people who love and support you or who are willing to help you at a moment's notice in your time of need– it would be sad. My passion is to inspire others to live an abundant life with a trustworthy and loving supported community network. It takes time, effort, and awareness, but it is never too late to begin.

Now that I have shared with you how we accidentally discovered our community of support, I would also like to share how you can purposely build one for yourself and your loved ones. There is never a better time to grow your network of support. I wholeheartedly believe that people who belong to a supportive community live their lives with joy, peace, happiness, security, love, and abundance! A life of real treasure! What more can one desire if one lives a life surrounded with such support and love?

Here are a few basic steps toward abundant living:

- First and foremost, develop self-love. Self-love alleviates turning to worldly things or harmful behavior to fill a void.
- Second, change your mindset. Abandon the "Me, me, me!" philosophy and embrace "We, we, we!" instead. Please open your eyes to opportunities to help others and contribute to their lives.
- Take the time to get to know your neighbors. Help new neighbors transition into your neighborhood. Show you care. Be a part of building a fantastic and friendly community.
- Support local small businesses around your community. They may have the opportunity to support you in your time of need.
- Join a club – Men/Women's Club, Hobby Club, Reading Club, Hiking Club, Sports Club, Creative Arts Club, and host activities outside the club. You will become an important part of each other's network.
- Take an interest in and assist your colleagues and co-workers when you can. Work will become more enjoyable, and you will collaborate when needed.
- Celebrate life! Acknowledge birthdays and special occasions and invite new friends to celebrate yours.
- Create a haven for youth in your home. Children and teens benefit from added love and support from their community. Moreover, be that loving and safe home in your community they will want to be around.

- Build a business networking group. A business networking group's value extends well beyond just business and can provide you with personal support along with ongoing business referrals during downtimes in life and industry.

Building communities of personal life support takes time and effort, and it starts with you. You must be willing to serve others and to be the community for others as you want them to become part of yours.

Some put a high priority on acquiring the best of the best in luxurious jewels, clothing, cars, homes, yachts, private jets, and other things that can seemingly provide pleasure or recognition. I see no fault in having those desires, wanting superior quality, and experiencing the excitement of what different things can bring into our lives. We experience joy and satisfaction of having riches and wealth for a moment, or maybe even continually, and there is nothing wrong with that. These are at the top of the list of what people want and strive for daily. However, let me ask you a question: When tragedy hits your life, what is it that you seek the most? Is it for you and your loved ones to have a nice car or home, fly in private jets, or be invited to lavish homes and parties? Probably not. Most would say they would want to live. They would wish their loved ones to live. To live with love, joy, health, happiness, wholeness, security, and abundance! Yes, of course, we yearn to live abundantly, but what does that mean? Abundant living involves a connection to a higher God and purpose, in a healthy state of mind, spirit, and body, surrounded by a caring community. That is what we want in the end; no longer would materialistic "showy" things satisfy us with death upon us. We know these things can bring pleasure, but they cannot provide us with true happiness. Contentment is the key to abundant living and having the support of a community that we treasure is a big part of this. Our priority now is for meaningful moments that we can cherish in our lives with those we care about– true treasures rather than temporary pleasures.

Earlier, I mentioned my mission was to impact many lives positively. I have lived that in many ways. Now, my mission is to help billions of parents and caregivers worldwide build a loving and supportive community for abundant living. The choice of abundant living is yours. You can decide to acquire things and make a great impression on others, and it is terrific if that brings you happiness. However, authentic, abundant living is in serving others. It is having peace of mind, being loved, having gratitude for others, and having a solid relationship with God – our miracle worker. Having a supportive community willing to give from their heart during your time of need is priceless. Show up, bless abundantly, and as discussed previously, The Bank of Providence will render returns. I had always felt that being generous and serving others brought me great joy and a sense of satisfaction. Little did I know that by doing so, I was making deposits into The Bank of Providence for withdrawals later in my life. It is the law of reciprocity spoken about in the Bible. I know it because I live in it, and you can live it too! THAT is the REAL treasure of life and the truest form of living abundantly.

"ACKNOWLEDGING THE GOOD THAT IS ALREADY IN YOUR LIFE IS THE FOUNDATION FOR ALL ABUNDANCE."

~ Eckhart Tolle

CHAPTER EIGHT

Life is an Initiation

By Sam Frazer

M y name is Sam Fraser, and I will be sharing my journey to abundant living throughout my lifetime. I am 32 years young. From growing up in uncertainty, violence, and much confusion from society's way of being, I struggled to manifest my dream reality through my unconscious awareness of my conditioning that limited my belief systems in many areas of my life. Four years ago, I had an awakening and transitioned from a stressed, lost soul working as a carpenter/builder contractor to now; new earth guide, intuitive mentor, healer, Chanel, multidimensional alchemist and 5D business owner where my team and I guide others throughout their awakening journey of rediscovery and empowerment for their soul-aligned purpose in life as way-showers for the safe and sacred evolution of humanity and mother earth's conscious rising.

I remember that we are all highly advanced streams of consciousness here for a human experience and are here for a series of INITIATIONS for our own unique and collective soul evolution. Initiations are stages of one's development through life that we have to pass to move onto the next phase of soul development.

Before we begin, I invite you to close your eyes and begin to take seven deep breaths, in through your nose and out through

111

your mouth. Firstly, feel, see, and sense a grounding cord connecting to your heart space as you follow it deep into mother earth's life force energy. Once you feel the warmth from mother earth's soothing red presence, begin seven deep, long, slow, intentional breaths, breathing in abundance and breathing out abundance in a balanced form of giving and receiving. With every breath, feel yourself drop deeper and deeper into the present moment of reciprocity.

Abundant Living

Hello dear one, I very much appreciate you dropping into this space and receiving. I will be channeling the majority of this chapter but will also be dropping into my human form for some lighthearted humor and humility.

I want to start by stating that abundance is not just a monetary gain but rather a collective vibration that runs throughout every area of our lives, creating our own unique personal energetic frequency of collective abundance. When we start to see each area of our life as a ball of energy that vibrates from 0-1000 Hz and beyond, we can then begin to break down each area and see which area of our lives needs more energy/attention. Please see the main areas of our lives;

- infinite/limitless potential
- relationships/ friendships
- love life/ sexual energy/ creation
- family/community/tribe
- money/currency
- career/purpose/mission
- gifts/services/abilities
- self-love/ worth/ image
- health/ mental /physical
- personal growth/emotional/spiritual

Each of these unique areas of life creates the collective abundance of your unique vibrational frequency of super abundance.

Abundance is our birthright as divine sovereign beings, and I am in no way stating that I have completed all the coded initiations of abundance. Instead, I have come so far in my journey embodying a certain vibrational frequency of abundance within all areas of my life, some of which have a higher vibrational frequency of abundance than others. Coded initiations are steps for one to embody in their lives to become a vibrational match to higher states of abundance frequency for each area. Codes are certain frequencies, ways of being, archetypes that one has embodied to hold that frequency of being and awareness. Once you have embodied a specific code, then you're able to deliver that code to others through an energetic exchange of frequencies through mentorship, spoken word transmissions, light language channeled through your art, sound, frequency, and vibration, which shifts their cells over time so that they are able to receive the codes and then begin the journey of embodying them as a daily practice to reprogram the neurological pathways and personal energetic frequency.

Examples of codes; archetypal codes such as the - King / Queen - Warrior / Warrior Goddess - Magician / Priestess - Lover / Healer are certain high vibrational ways of being where one has embodied the energetics of these states of being.

Codes for values once embodied; integrity - compassion - transparency - honor - humility - truth - compassion - empathy - discernment - laughter/play - love - leaning the fuck in are some of the core values that I am continually embodying more of which will differ for each human being.

Over the past few years, I have been channeling remembrance codes; these are coded messages from my ancient past awoken from my cellular memory through receiving these messages in dreams, plant-based medicine journeys or through my higher self. It is shown that there are many levels of coded frequencies that we must embody before we can transition and morph into the next higher state of abundance frequency. There are many stages of abundance to embody from my awareness, and you cannot skip anyone. Each is an initiation, a test for you to hold that vibration/feeling of abundance in your thoughts, feelings, body, cells, and beliefs. This way, when you embody your beliefs around abundant living, you will match the frequency and attract a vibrational match of what you hold in your cells and beliefs through the Law of Attraction – Like A Like Attraction. Scientifically, when we begin to clear present life trauma, past life trauma and ancestral trauma, negative programs, mannerisms, traits, beliefs from our cells we begin to vibrate at a higher frequency towards love and empowerment without the negative programming from society and trauma that has been passed down from our ancestral DNA or experienced in our lifetime. We begin to magnetically attract more abundant opportunities and people that match the frequency of our own unique personal energetic frequency, vision, goals and personality. When we are negative and have many unsuppressed emotions, we will keep attracting similar people and situations in life that will trigger these emotions, allowing an opportunity for you to feel and heal the emotions that arise.

Over the following few pages, I will deliver a series of transmissions that I have been downloading over the last four years from my awakening journey for how to live an abundant life that is deeply rooted in trust, calm, safety, ease, grace, and flow.

I have decided to take this opportunity to write this chapter within this book as I feel it will play an integral part in the collective consciousness shift on how we can see abundance in our lives. I hope it will help us all live out our birthright as sovereign beings living within our fullest expression playing out our purpose and mission here on earth. Living our true purpose ultimately leads to an abundance of happiness. Co-writing this book is an aligned initiation for myself, which will help me shift into a higher self-worth state for my next stage of abundant living. When we follow our intuition, we are aligned with our soul's truest purpose. Our mission is to stay in our lane, focused on what is suitable for us and our aligned growth for expansion. Initiations are stages in your life that you have to move through to learn certain lessons in life to embody more of who you are holding that in your energy field, creating more abundance and freedom within your life. The game of evolution and expansion. Cool hey!

As was stated many times already, there are certain initiations we all have to go through in life to learn lessons so we can remember and embody the energetics of our stages of evolution and abundant living. All are explained below.

The Human Experience - Soul Advancement

Let's start this transmission with this: we have all lived many lifetimes before, if not thousands for some. There are beginner souls and advanced souls. We have come to earth to learn the lessons that we did not learn this last lifetime and lessons of initiations that we have created with our soul groups before we reincarnate back for the human experience once again. The human experience is always programmed from our own soul's free will, and we all have the choice to take part in the game of soul evolution or not. Soul groups are certain stages of evolution in the spirit realm where when we pass/die, we incarnate back to the source and connect with our soul groups and guides. This is where we reconnect and then choose our desired life to reincarnate back to earth when ready to initiate ourselves back into the human experience for more development and evolution.

The fullest and purest expression of abundance is source consciousness itself. That is what I feel we are all transitioning towards - high energized crystalline frequencies of pure abundance within every cell of our physical and energetic bodies. Freedom.

By the way, how frickin exciting is this human experience? We get to eat food and feel our emotions! Yeowwww!

We have recently come to the end of a 26,000-year cycle. We have now entered the golden age, the Age of Aquarius, where the Schumann resonance, which measures the earth's electromagnetic frequency of the planet's collective consciousness energy field, shifted from 8 Hz to 38 Hz on the 21st of December 2020. This is all happening naturally from the consistent solar flare flashes entering the earth's atmosphere creating waves of high vibrational 5D and above crystalline frequencies that are rippling throughout our collective consciousness and awakening our cellular memory of suppressed and repressed emotions of wisdom codes that have been lying dormant for many lifetimes and beyond. Ancient wisdom codes are forgotten ways of being lying dormant within our DNA that we can unlock through a series of healing practices and initiations. We have lived many lifetimes, and throughout the start of time, we were pure beings with no programs from society or control methods. Unfortunately, throughout time, we have been negatively programmed and controlled via systems and elite members of society for greed and control methods to infiltrate our DNA cellular structure to keep us dulled down. We are suppressed through manipulation via advertising, TV CONTROLLER, news and media through our subconscious minds. The level of control and deceit is mind-boggling!

Take some long, deep, slow, intentional breaths and allow this all to settle into your being.

We are made up of 70% of water, meaning we are malleable. When we are around higher vibrational frequencies, such as other high vibes humans of embodied levels of abundance and coded frequencies, we can all shift into that higher state of vibrational frequency through mirroring their behaviors and energy. We live within a holographic universe, meaning we are all reflections of each other. We are all co-creating the collective consciousness and expansion of humanity and mother earth's evolution from our current vibrational frequency and beliefs. This is why it's so important to do the work in decoding our cellular DNA from past life, ancestry, present life trauma, programs that are limiting our abundance in all areas of our life. Whatever we hold within our cells of beliefs is ultimately the reality that is reflected to us. This is why the elite members who control our world like to control our beliefs and way of thinking through subtle subconscious programming to control the entire collective consciousness.

Multidimensional alchemy allows us to cancel and clear all lineages from all timelines, dimensions, and realities, from upline, downline, and sidelines of our cellular memory, which ultimately removes and makes room for our cellular memory to be awoken. Your wisdom codes have been deactivated due to generations of control and suppression. Upline lineage is our parents, ancestral and past life DNA – Downline is our own and our children's DNA – Sideline is our cousin's DNA lineage. When we do the healing on ourselves, we can heal our ancestors, our past lives trauma, our cousins, and our future children's bloodline so that it is clear and free from negative attachments from the generations of negative programming. When we do the work on ourselves, the cycle stops with us healing our family's bloodline and lineages. Therefore, we are purer in our DNA and every cell in our body. Free from trauma and negative programs, beliefs that have been subconsciously programmed into us for thousands of years. We then become more abundant in every area of our lives. Epic!

The Power of Sexual Energy and Creation

Sexual energy is directly linked to and matches the exact vibrational frequency of creation. Our sexual energy has been purposely dulled down by society's deep-rooted programming that suppresses our power of creation through deluded expectations of sexual encounters through the porn industry's allusions. One must learn to cultivate their chi (energy) back into the body through regulated and intentional breathing. This will amplify your creativity, allowing you to attract more abundance within your life. Just setting the intention every morning and before you go to bed to breathe in your sexual energy up and around your body for creation purposes will activate this process. When practiced with a sexual partner, you're able to reach altered states of consciousness where sexual trauma can be released with love, safety, and liberation. Sex magic is a potent exercise to enhance and amplify your collective manifestations for your sacred union or personal endeavors.

I have decided to give you this knowledge now to prepare you for the latter part of this chapter, where I will be sharing some key insights on how you can surrender to your divinely or-chestrated initiations in this lifetime where you can stay in your lane and pass the initiations that life throws your way. Remember that the Universe, Source, God is working for you, not against you and that there are always gifts and lessons within the pain that you may encounter through the aligned experiences you move through in life. We all have created sit-uations in life at the soul level to learn the lessons. If one chooses not to learn the lesson involved within the initiation, one will keep attracting a similar experience until one has felt the emotions involved and passed the test. Take a look back at your life now and see how every experience led you to be-come who you are today. All unconscious beliefs and trauma have to be alchemized to experience the freedom of pure tao abundance.

With all that said, I hope you're enjoying the journey so far.

My Journey and Experience

I will now be dropping in with my personal, transparent expe-rience on how I cultivated a certain level of abundance over the last four years from transitioning from a carpenter builder who was chasing money, toys, women, drugs, and anything external to fulfil the void that I felt every day. See, I was al-ways chasing something, never present, always doing and never really just BEING.

I am now the co-founder of Flow Tribe, a self-development movement and the founder of Warrior Flow created for Men and Women with my Queen Yani Foord. Both creations were birthed with the vision to guide and awaken millions of souls into their purpose, passion, and mission, where we all live abundantly, thriving within our gifts and intuitive abilities helping the world evolve organically, prosperously, and freely.

You have heard the term initiation a lot already, and there is a reason for that. Everything in life is an initiation. Certain levels are coded frequencies to embody, which allow you to shift into that higher state of abundance. When you are intuitively guided by spirit to work through your initiations in each area of your life, this will allow you to amplify and accelerate your collective abundance vibration for all areas of your life, shifting you into a higher state of abundance. I know this because I remember and have experienced this in other lifetimes and this life also.

Every time you step further into a more expressed version of you, where you are embodying more of who you are beneath all the veils, masks and fake facades that society has programmed us to wear, the more self-worth you will have to embody into every cell of your being. Because I am shifting at such a rapid velocity, I constantly move through self-worth levels to receive the higher frequencies of abundance for my birthright. When we start to let go of who we think we are and really surrender to what we truly are as multidimensional sovereign beings that can access the highest vibrations of abundance in all areas of life, many doubts and fears will begin to creep in. This is when you need to move through the resistance of fear and become friends with it while enjoying the ride along the way. Easier said than done, right?

Firstly, we must surrender to what is for us now and be open to receive what is for us now. The more we fight or hold on, the more resistance occurs, and you will keep attracting the same scenarios in life until you learn the lessons and pass that initiation. Understanding the ego-mind is paramount to notice when he plays out. When we can detach ourselves from the control aspect of the ego-mind, then we will be fully free. The ego-mind is solely here to protect you and keep you safe, but unfortunately, he goes above and beyond his job title, keeping you suppressed in your comfort zones. My ego still plays out, but because I have an awareness of my ego, I can nip it in the bud and continue the journey of being free without too much control from him. It's a journey for sure, which I am still moving through.

When we start to drop deep into the body of trust, safety, calm, and relaxation, then we can begin the transition into abundant living through the power of breath. Breathe in abundance and breathe out abundance in a balanced form of giving and receiving. This allows the heart space to stay balanced and in love because integrity is love and abundance is all around us.

I spent many years healing my inner child, my core wounds from my mum and my dad, my relationship with my ego, along with ancestral lineages that had been passed down through my bloodline into my cellular DNA structure. And I am in no way finished yet. I have surrendered to the infinite and limitless possibilities of potentialities and that I do not know; instead, I just remember what has been forgotten and suppressed. I do not force my healing journey nor rush it. Spirit, my higher self, very much guides me and intuitively gives me a nudge when I need to lean the fuck in and shift through programs that no longer serve me within my stage of embodiment. A high vibrational community of like-minded tribes is required to shift progressively into an empowered, abundant state of being where you are all able to invite in conversations of truth that illuminate and evoke blind spots that one is not able to foresee, process, let go and transmute. The ego will do all in its power to protect you from the truth, for you to fully surrender, admit and take full ownership of unconscious patterns that are playing out through the shadow self. This is why mentorship, shadow work is so important to lean into, love and transmute.

Intuitive Abilities - Super Powers

How one can intuitively foresee their journey of aligned or-chestrated lessons of initiations that one must move through is through activating their clairvoyant abilities. These are our in-tuitive senses that can be activated by deepening our connec-tion with our emotions and sensitivity and learning the aligned lessons in life. They are clairvoyance - clairknowing - clairsentience and clairaudience.

Clairvoyance is the ability to see and communicate with spirit guides or see into our aligned future.

Clairknowing is the ability to follow our inner gut instinct of knowing something will happen. You might get that inner sense that something will play out, and then boom, it does.

Clairsentience is the ability to feel and sense something hap-pening or to experience future premonitions as they are actu-ally happening, allowing you to stay in alignment with your initiations, stages of life's lessons for your soul evolution.

Clairaudience is the ability to channel wisdom, guidance, or future timeline events through hearing the whispers of your higher self or other higher dimensional beings offering support or mentorship.

I have activated all of my Clair abilities to a certain level by learning many lessons and experiencing my aligned initiations early in my awakening journey. When you do so, you are re-warded with your intuitive gifts. All these abilities are para-mount in staying on track while receiving aligned messages and information, helping you evolve within your designated stages of development that you had already created before you reincarnated back to earth, as we all choose our parents, les-sons, and people who we connect with for our human experi-ence so we can evolve organically staying true to our path!

From my personal experience, it has been the gift of stepping out of mind and into my body, heart cultivating these gifts even more. Having a deep practice in connecting to my higher self through meditation practice, breath work, and other multidimensional practices allows me to ultimately feel my emotions to enhance my sensitivity to feel more within me and around me.

However, from the very start of my journey and still, to this day, I outsource other humans for intuitive reads on my current energy field that helps me stay on track for my soul purpose alignment. I am meticulous; I do not skip my initiations that I need to embody, and I am surrounded by many highly gifted beings, which makes the journey flow with ease and grace. I also use energy cards to help me stay on track and have regular readings connecting into my higher self to receive messages that help me stay on my aligned path in life.

So, I'm guessing you're probably wondering how abundant I am in this present moment?

The only area of my life that is "not yet" overflowing with abundance is my vibrational frequency with my self-worth charging for my services, which also affects my V.F for currency/money/prosperity attraction and is something I am currently moving through. Many of us who have ancestral programs deep-rooted around slavery via the monastery system will carry this forward into their present life. I have been releasing eons of suppressed slavery codes from my DNA over the last year through many types of healing modalities. "I AM WORTHY TO BE PAID ABUNDANTLY FOR MY SERVICES" is something I say to myself on repeat. I have been diving deep into changing my language and beliefs around money for some time; they are the toughest programs that I have moved through, along with my sexual trauma and body shame. The more I step into my power, the more self-worth I have to embody, which allows me to feel worthy within integrity to charge for my services. This is why multidimensional healing is so powerful as we can clear eons of suppressed programs limiting our abundance within money/currency, which is directly linked to self-worth and love. In most of our realities, money is needed. We use money as a means to exchange for products and services. Most things we have, have been paid for with the energy of money; food, clothes, blankets, home, cars, holidays, self-development, and so on. Currency has been around for thousands of years. Money is simply a reciprocal exchange between parties to measure the value of one's services and products. It is a byproduct of the services and products we offer. And when we become a vibrational match to our soul's worth to be of service for this world in what we offer, we will then attract our perfect soul-aligned tribe, students to work and co-create with, as they will be attracted to our truth of worthiness for who we are and what we're worth and valued. We are drawn to truth, integrity, and humility.

I do not have 1000's in my bank account as I do not hoard money. I am always investing in myself, Flow Tribe, life's experiences, and our community expansion. I drink high vibrational Kangen water and eat organic, locally sourced vegetables. I have a beautiful home with 800 sq ft of garden and lush grass surrounded by a whole tribe of new earth leaders, all impacting this world. Money comes in ebbs and flows and moves through my life gracefully. As I came to finish the first draft for this chapter, I had a massive win in becoming a vibrational match to my worth and what I should be charging to match my energy exchange through the services that I offer. I tripled my six-month mentorship immersion because it was my vibrational match for the embodied value I serve. When I felt and transmuted the feelings that were blocking me from feeling worthy of being in this match, I instantly had a brother, who I didn't even know, contact me the next day and sign up for my 6-month mentorship immersion. I have three more aligned men who are eager to work with me as well. Now that's Magic.

Just remember, you can only create abundance from FEEL-ING abundant already, and I do. I feel rich, like a millionaire. This is my current INITIATION stage, embodying the feeling of abundance in every cell of my being. From this state of being, I can create deep trust and safety within my nervous system, which has allowed me to feel abundant, free, and thrives with what I have in my life right now. This is my current initiation, and all the deep work that we have done is paying off. We have created and birthed all our new offerings for the next four months. We will be launching our seven-week "Initiate & Integrate" in-person Immersion next month with an expected exchange of $60 thousand dollars landing in our bank account from the services we love creating and facilitating. Now that's something to celebrate, right…!

I have the firm belief that when money is used with integrity, it can change the world. So, I will continue to invest the money that I create (not earn) into Flow Tribe's personal development, as it's our birthright to have abundance, and money/currency is a tool that helps us CREATE that reality creating real change for our world.

Here are some of my favorite methods for creating abundance within my life:

Gratitude

It doesn't matter where you are in your life in terms of abundance, pain, trauma, confusion, or depression. You have a choice to change the way you think and feel around what you have already within your life. Embodying the vibrational feeling of GRATITUDE for everything big and small within your life is a must. Affirmations on your walls, around your house, recorded empowering affirmations spoken with your voice with intentional energy are super powerful also.

TRUST Cultivating deep trust that the universe is working FOR YOU - with you, not against you or to you. It can be a tricky reality to understand when shit is hitting the fan but trust me, I have been there, and this was one of my all-time faves for allowing the abundant flow of the universe to give me exactly what is for me. Through this awareness, you can see the gift in every situation that you're in and learn the lessons along the way.

Boundaries

Surround yourself with high vibrational loving souls who wish to see you rise and who are always there to spur you on with integral heart-centered encouragement. This may mean you have to disconnect from many friendships to protect your energy or self-worth and sovereignty. Creating boundaries built upon your fundamental values in life is paramount to raising your vibration and living your truth.

Values

Some of my favorite values are integrity, transparency, unity, love, community, compassion, fun, laughter, play, discernment, leaning the fuck in, honor and humility. These have helped me stay true to myself and my path by embodying these coded values' energetics'.

Feel Abundant Now

Start feeling abundant now. AFFIRM: "I AM A LIMITLESS INFINITE BEING WHO IS ABUNDANT IN EVERY CELL OF MY PHYSICAL AND SUBTLE BODY." We attract what we feel within our heart space, so start feeling SUPER ABUNDANT NOW!

Money/Currency

Love money and currency like you love everything else like you love every area of your life, and you will attract more of it. When we match the frequency of what we desire, we cannot help but become a vibrational match. Therefore, we will call in and attract more opportunities to receive money/currency in all possibilities and circumstances that we encounter. Ultimately it all comes down to the WORTH that you hold in your heart. Affirm - "I AM WORTHY TO BE AND HAVE IT ALL." When we embody the highest vibration of worthiness and the feeling of having it all, true freedom, then we will attract that frequency back into our reality. For myself and my Queen, we have spent four years embodying our worth to charge for our services as we are worthy of service for humanity and mother earth. All the internal work that we have done and continue to play in, along with the state of worth we feel in our hearts and the integrity we hold in our being, is now attracting our soul-aligned tribe who is investing heavily into Flow Tribe experiences, offerings, and services. It feels GREAT! Co-creation baby!

Giving And Receiving

Keeping a balanced form of giving and receiving - input and output into the heart space, always being of service when your cup is full. Your intention is everything, so be very aware of blind spots and unconscious core wounds that might affect your level of integrity and intention for your truth. Everyone can feel one's level of integrity. If one is coming from wounded projections, then it's vital to alchemize core wounds from mum, dad, and any trauma so that others can feel your deep trust of integral service and deep-felt intentions. Give for the right reasons.

Invest In Yourself

You are number one; putting yourself first is not selfish, but it is how you're able to serve at a higher level. This is why intuitive spirit-guided mentorship is essential for one's journey so that you're able to be held throughout, transmuting your core wounds as a child into light, deleting programs that no longer serve you, awakening your forgotten empowered beliefs in every area of your life. This results in attracting more abundance into every area of your life as you have cultivated that empowering abundant energy from within, your internal self, which ultimately reflects outwards, creating your external world where you begin to impact everyone around you.

I want to finish this chapter by aligning the importance of alchemizing and transmuting one's beliefs towards the highest form of worth for abundant living, which to me is freedom. To be free in all ones being so one can experience the true abundance of freedom within every cell of our body is our birthright as sovereign beings.

So much love, Fam!

Keep leaning in and having fun along the way.

And remember, your state of abundant living is your choice, so don't let anybody tell you any different. We all have the free will to live how we desire and that can be different from your neighbor, and that's ok.

"FEAR OF THE FUTURE MAKES PEOPLE SETTLE FOR THINGS IN THE PRESENT THAT COMPLETELY DEFY ABUNDANT LIVING."

~ Beth Moore

CHAPTER NINE

Waves of Awareness, Intention, Action Undercurrent; A Whole New World of Holistic Wealth

By Catherine Kavadas

Aloha Lui Noa. My name is Catherine Kavadas from Australia.

Whether you were drawn to John Spender's philanthropic efforts in Bali *or* you were drawn to this series because you want to manifest small or large *changes* in your life in this fast-paced new world, *or* even if you have it all and want to know what is next for you in your journey to fulfilment, welcome.

What is the distinction between the beings who manifest Abundant Living and stretch beyond and those that do not?

The answer and the framework of this chapter is **Awareness, Intention,** and strategic, constant, and consistent daily **Action**.

These three elements are necessary to bring forth and expose your truth of invisible beliefs, limiting patterns, self-sabotage, self-doubt, fears and unconscious blocks to your human potential.

Whether your life has been plagued by hardship *or* filled with an overflow of experiences of love and compassion and or a combination of both up to now, every single human being will face their adversity. By choosing awareness by design, paying attention to life, and the truth of the situation, you become better able to understand a situation.

We all have the ability to live a life that is an example, the ability to accept where you are and shift focus by humbly asking better questions to locate the benefits and the gifts; asking these questions is the difference between a life of success and a life of suffering.

This allows the creative opportunity to practice a moment to moment your best focus, advocating your best influence, a conscious awareness in the preparation tending to your accomplishment and maintenance of your vibrational atmosphere and your vibrational alignment of who you are.

A receptive mode of non-physical source energy moving around and through your physical body, in your powerful NOW, with that all-knowing, omniscient non-physical source energy, that there is always some value in what is happening.

Tending to your environments, receiving and encouraging wonderful things, guiding yourself back to a state of natural well-being.

Being in that state of well-being, advocating for yourself, is answering a higher call, which means self-loving behaviors, be nice to yourself, quiet your mind, rest well, eat well, surround yourself with beautiful things, play with fun people, a genuine compliment in the right place, thoughts that are uplifting of self and others, engaging in activities that feel good, watch movies that are uplifting to your human spirit.

This focus energetically assists with exposing shadows, releasing patterns that no longer serve, helping accelerate healing of self, the planet and others.

Unless you have a process to awaken the part of you that has the desire to grow and contribute, you could go to your grave, never fulfilling the path you were meant to fulfil.

As I write this chapter, our planet is in the middle of a pandemic with the name COVID-19.

Depending on where you reside, there is either unification and a leader focusing on healing or a leader focusing on dividing through fear and a construct of scarcity.

Constant shifts of truths and untruths being shared across various platforms about the pandemic, politics, global markets, massive fires, floods, earthquakes, natural disasters, riots and rallies have sidelined some people and allowed others to step into prosperity.

For some, COVID-19 has caused a spectrum of *dis-stress*, leading to anxiety, depression, increased suicide cases, massive upheaval in global markets, disruptions of all sorts, job loss, divorce, and death of loved ones. For others, the pandemic has brought *you-stress*, leading to prosperity, growth, new skills, new awareness, deep clearing, deep healing, deeper understandings, and bonding with their families, experiencing *A Journey Of Riches* and abundant living in a profound way.

A Personal Story to Share

For 30 years, I lived in a construct of awareness called *sufficient living*, followed by two years in a construct called *scarcity living,* then back to *sufficient living* again before consciously placing myself in an environment with students, teachers and masters who demonstrate the construct and possibilities of *abundant living*.

It started with a spectrum of darkness, an existence of self-sabotage, sleep walking of sorts, with strange and unfamiliar, unpleasant, heavy feelings. I felt shut down, numb, desensitized, and disassociated from the essence of beauty that once was everywhere. I felt heavy, exhausted, unfulfilled and stressed.

I had a lot of good things going for me; I was born in Australia, middle-class and privileged. I completed high school as school captain with many scholastic awards, recognized citizenship, attended university and completed a double degree (Commerce/Law) made some really great friendships, memories and experiences. I married my childhood sweetheart (while I am writing this, we are still choosing each other 26 years later). I practiced law, travelled and reached a point where I was earning six figures; we had our first child, built our first home. People were in and out of our home all the time, weekend BBQs, parties, family holidays.

It was moving forward until it wasn't.

Stress can, in fact, be a *stimulus for change.*

Some of the greatest leaders talk about the benefits of stress to build your resilience, the benefits for growth; they also speak that *NOT* all stresses are the same.

For me to explain this personal story at a very basic level, let me clarify the two kinds of stress.

One type is called *dis-stress,* a stress not by design, default or inertia. It can stem from completing tasks that are not in alignment with your values and highest priorities. *Dis-stress* causes you to exist, grounded in a construct of scarcity; it is a state that is not constructive, resisting life, disharmony with life, worst-case scenario future event that has not occurred as yet. For me, it was constraining; the external voices were louder than my internal voice, my spirit felt drained, I gained weight, and I felt disconnected from my higher self.

The second type is called *you-stress*, a stress and pressure by design through strategic action that is aligned with your vision, values, mission and purpose. This alignment to your vision helps fuel you into living. The living is grounded in a construct of sufficiency, the hurdles you experience lead to fulfilment, you understand adversity presents itself by design for growth and greater contribution; you welcome exhaustion, you have rituals, practices, habits, tools in your own designer tool belt that help you with rest and recovery to emerge stronger as you strengthen the muscle of resilience. You are freer, lighter, letting go of weight, and more fun; your internal voice, your guidance system will present itself and the external noise seemingly to distract you from your truth and path will be revealed for what it is. It can at times still be heard and gets cleared with waves of eternal self - compassion, ease, pure love, unconditional healing, guidance and inner peace, knowing that everything is working for you.

Dis-stress and Construct of Scarcity Living

Under the pressure of *dis-stress*, I entered a scarcity living construct, which manifested in a variety of ways; **cloudy mind, guarded heart, and unhealthy gut.**

It came to a head over the end of the year, that period when Australia has public holidays between Dec and Jan 2008-2009. For me, the turning point looked like this. I was standing at the sink in the kitchen of our beautiful newly built home. My husband Alex and our then two years old daughter Christina were eating dinner, and I was washing my plate. Our daughter turned to my husband and said:

135

"Where is mummy, daddy? I cannot find her!"

Alex looked at our child, perplexed too, as I looked at him.

"I am here, Christina," I shouted. "Who asked you to say that?" I yelled.

She just looked at Alex, heard nothing from my lips, standing only a meter away, yelling.

"Where is my mummy, daddy?" "I cannot find my mummy!" "I lost my mummy!"

She was two; there could have been many reasons why she said what she said and why she could not hear me despite my shouting, waving my arms and signaling I'M HERE.

Tears started to pour, tears that continued to flow for two days.

Five doctors, five different labels - none diagnosing symptoms or getting to the root cause. I was left with no relief, confusion, frustration, agitation, anger, despondency, despair, and a desperation for answers.

I was unequipped for that manifestation of my scarcity construct.

In the spirit of honesty and transparency, when I looked in the **mirror naked** at the end of 2008/2009, I truly, deeply and wholeheartedly did not love or respect myself. The reflection showed a very unbalanced self, all externally focused, referential, and conditional.

For the purposes of this chapter, an orientation to *Journey of Riches abundant living*, I was focused in that two years on financial freedom. All external referential manifestations, actions, practices, focuses were attached to material acquisitions, which resulted in the other spheres of my life becoming bankrupt.

I was not self-aware; I was unaware of the dance between the internal and external world, I was unaware of who I was at a deep core level, unaware of the necessity of personal leadership mastery, self- values, self-habits, self-rituals, self-education, conscious environments by choice, unaware of the five stages of manifestation taught by *Regan Hillyer*, unaware of my subconscious programming, the importance of environments such as *Neurogym* – unaware, unaware, unaware.

To fully understand the wisdom of what feels like a patch of darkness, a spectrum of darkness, a season of hail, a storm in the ocean of abundance with a practice of releasing resistance – this can be the universes' benevolence pointing the "I" in the new direction.

Awareness of a spectrum of perceived darkness to seeing the gift where you are not okay with people and circumstances, a perceived threat to reveal what work is to be done on where you are not free: a guide to adopting a growth mindset, unguarded heart, and healthy gut with the *intention* as feedback to give self-permission to embrace life and release tension and friction instead of creating resistance. Whatever is happening, can I stay still, centered, in peace, guided forward movements towards the light, a force for good and goodness, a rebirth, a real sense of commitment to living an extraordinary life while simultaneously fully accepting where you are and the way things are? Can I be with this? Truly and deeply, am I ok with this?

Darkness can be a teacher of sorts, calling you to shift resistance to freedom and bring forth a manifestation of vitality.

You-stress and Construct of Sufficiency Living the A Journey of Riches and Abundant Living

Under pressure, *you-stress* helps you to develop the muscle of your self-awareness.

How did I make the transition from ***dis-stress to you-stress***?

On the 6th January 2009, I was 32 years of age, and it was the first such profound revelation.

The wake-up call helped me embrace the miracle of constant change that would fill and fuel my life from that date forward. An awareness at that stage of my journey to educate myself on my three brains that of ***head, heart and gut.***

The head brain has most of the chemicals that are paramount for our experience of the world.

It is the seat of logic and intellect, with the unconscious mind (the elephant) directing around 90%-95% of our behaviors and the conscious mind (the ant) directing 5-10% of our behaviors. There are multiple parts to our brains: including the crocodile survival part of our brain and the emotional, "I want to belong", monkey mind where emotions reside to better understand our shared humanity. Then there is the executive center, a more evolved part of the brain, the seat of creativity and problem-solving intelligence, only living by the highest set of values; what lights up is evident in their own independent, healthy judgements.

Intention and setting an intention lights up the part of the brain called the reticular activating system, which helps attract things that are most relevant to your intention.

The heart brain and feelings allow you to co-create a vortex of joy, consisting of neural pathways running from the heart to the head brain and the head brain to the heart.

The gut brain produces 90% of the body's serotonin, which is involved in mood and emotional management. This is why caring for your gut is important to your overall well-being. When you eat well, you feel well.

Grateful for my wake-up call and appreciative of the message, I created an intention to make meaningful changes in my life which I manifested in a series of daily actions. Every day from 2009-2012, I would start my morning with a line, a story, something from the bible. I would fill my day with what bought joy to my heart. In the beginning, there were three simple things that bought joy to my heart that I did over and over:

Hugs and rumbles on a Sunday morning with hubby and our child;

A long hot bath every night after work to release tension and wash sensitivities away;

Sand beneath my feet and between my toes;

These moments, these experiences helped me focus more and more on my self-loving, compassionate question. *What brings joy to my heart?* The awareness of this question, the focus allows a journey to start that is beyond what I held in my awareness at that point.

A sufficiency construct showed up in my direct experience living well and without regrets. Boundaries clear, needs known, communication direct; you are decisive, you have the spiritual faculty, strength, willingness, ability and freedom to live well, having a deep knowing and truth by living well you die well.

Bringing your reticular activating system to focus on questions such as;

- Am I doing what I love?
- What are my values?

- Do I know my truth?
- Do I know myself?
- What do I want?
- Am I demonstrating my values through my actions?
- Am I spending my time with those I value?
- Are my moments bringing joy to my heart?
- What do I love to do in my life that can also serve people?
- What are the 1-3 highest priority actions to make this happen daily?

In a sufficiency construct, you decide on what you want and what you don't want, what works and what doesn't work. By setting the intention on what brings joy to your heart, you learn how to keep the door open to wonder, astonishment, awe, bewilderment towards understanding your calling to the most meaningful pursuit the purpose of your soul-set.

You-stress helps in the construct of sufficiency living. As an appreciation for stress, it helps your viewpoint, helps your focus, helps the benefits, blessings, lessons, attention to realize that you are receiving a signal for change. At times it could be a change in your attitude, change in your vision, change in your viewpoint, change in your lifestyle choices, or a change in your resourcefulness, causing you to adjust.

You-stress is your partner in building resilience.

Sufficiency is the base camp where gratitude truly and deeply becomes a habit experienced with those practices, habits, rituals, tools and activations.

You-stress is the guide that challenges and supports you in your transition to abundant living with all its glory, flavors, colors and manifestations.

Construct of Abundant Living

By standing on the shoulders of giants, through receiving the gifts of their wisdom, some through live demonstrations in environments, some through direct experience of my own life, I am able to stand tall and see a whole new world.

Abundant living manifests when your highest values and priorities are in alignment with your behaviors. It is what happens when you use your **Awareness, Intention, and Action** towards Spiritual, Emotional, Mental, and Physical life experiences integrated holistically with your two worlds and integrated with your truth, the truth of pure love - a thread that connects us all.

Abundant living is a wisdom and internal knowing that the eternal moment is that only of the present moment. All we have is the Now. An empowered - presence is recognizing how every moment is here to help. Everything is choice, based on moment to moment, deliberate decisions.

A small domino, each meal of nourishing fresh nutrients brings a blessing not to be taken for granted. Easy access to fresh produce foundationally manifests better, healthier cells.

Expressing this truth fundamentally is eat well to feel well.

If you are open to living *A Journey Of Riches Abundant Living*, when people act lovingly in your presence, you sense that source energy, and it invites you to cultivate higher frequencies of light, and at that moment a miracle is taking form.

If you are open to *A Journey Of Riches Abundant Living*, you are always free to exit to a place of greater safety and help transform each drama cycle through demonstration of your word, strength and stronger practice of intention for that eternal moment, where we find our love for ourselves, our needs clear, and our boundaries defined.

If you are open to *A Journey Of Riches Abundant Living* for spirit faculty to grow and for growth and contribution to expand and evolve a willingness to face adversity, constant change, with the ability to recognize when to spend time feeling shut down, just to cultivate the strength, courage, tenacity and compassion to open back up more radiant, renewed, purified, powerful, love, loved; this helped me to understand how deep a reconstruction is under way for all who *choose* to heal themselves and do the deep inner work of *respect.*

When the wisdom of anger is acknowledged with the muscle of *self-awareness,* our spiritual faculty begins to recognize sensitivities, behaviors, masks, and signs for the awaking process that is underway, an expansion that has overwhelmed their innocence. Pure love or compassion in that moment is to offer space to others so they may process their feelings and remain open to an engagement, an invitation, an offering with consideration.

A smile, a celebration of untainted innocent hearts, freedom shining out from our eternally liberated nature. A smile signifies to another awake being - I am here, I matter, I exist for a reason, I am gifting you emotional generosity. A smile is a high-five exchange between earth angels. It is a remembrance of heaven on this earth, the purest space within us that awakes the purity of all. It is a small domino, a small goodwill offering that ripples across the universe.

If you have reached abundant living holistically, your visions will be expanding to becoming a visionary encompassing towards a mission for the eternal collective consciousness and the pure love soul-set revolution. Wow.

A Personal Story to Share

I have both experienced and observed the grieving process from conception and during the pandemic.

From conception birthed from love, through love, I am love and loved truly and deeply.

My maternal grandmother, who is one of my heroes, lost her only son, my mum and aunty's brother (my uncle Bill passed away on Mother's Day of 1977). He was at the ripe young age of 21, succumbing to a heart condition that Dr. Victor Chang found the cure to a short time later.

My mother at the time was four months pregnant with me.

Loss of a child / sibling / loved one brings with it challenges, obstacles, a sadness, a spectrum of grief that is very subjective dependent on several variables. There can be big traditional rituals around grief, such as funerals, when public occasions are over, life goes on for everyone else, while it might feel as if life has stopped and is out of control for the parents, grandparents, siblings, close family and friends.

When I was born, my maternal grandmother was five months deep in grief, and she shared her dominating thoughts to God during that period - why not take her, in place of her 21 years old son, who was filled with goodness and light.

My mum could not connect with such thoughts. Her viewpoint, her perspective, her chosen deliberate visualization, her feelings, her strategy, her open, loving heart, and her vision were operating from a different vibration, variance, a different frequency and vibrational values alignment. When sadness would come up for my mum, she would release those emotions with compassion, honor, love and hope.

My grandmother was operating from the survival part of her brain, the amygdala, the crocodile brain, the fear center - the most primitive part of the brain, any movement involved either food to eat or a predator primitive reactivity to attack, fueled by worry, stress, and pressure. In contrast, my mum was operating from the neo cortex the executive center part of her brain.

My grandmother was operating from a *dis-stress construct of scarcity living;* my mother was operating and demonstrating behaviors from *you-stress construct of sufficiency living.*

On my Christening day, my mother asked my grandmother for two things. To be as *present* to the moments of the sacrament, and to *not* wear black - a symbol, a ritual, a practice in my grandmother's culture to signify mourning.

On the day of my Christening, my grandmother made the decision to show up wearing a dark shade of grey; that day, my grandmother decided and chose to participate in the Christening and start participating in life again. It was a small domino, a small shift, moving her needle forward.

Victoria, our fourth child who has completed our nuclear family, is named in my grandmother's honor, signifying the love, respect and connection we share.

My parents have gone on to live their designed best lives, experiencing travel in their retirement, eight grandchildren to date from three daughters all alive, all independent thinkers, all loving women in their own right, mothers, leaders in their respective fields and roles.

My grandmother, now 80 years around the sun, raised herself from the ashes of immense pain a void filled with despair, to a force that learned to dig deep daily for the hope, gratitude, daily beauty, love, light, peace and joy she once lived knew and felt. Those foreign feelings transmuted into pure love. With that pure love, she transitioned from a *construct of scarcity living* to *sufficiency living* until she was ready to build an abundant life. When ready, she deliberately decided to build a business. She was the mastermind behind a subdivision in the '80s, and with that pure love, has built six units in a beautiful touristic island of Greece and is a great grandmother of thirteen.

My sister-in-law has been a hero in her own independence, a mother who experienced fear, despair, despondency and deep sadness upon the arrival of the news of her son's death in Jan 2020 in one moment, with one phone call, everything spinning out of control. Despite her doubts, concerns, questions, insecurities, she chose to live more in her soul-set, her inner victim transformed into her redeeming hero, a life of greater purpose being guided by a higher self for a greater legacy #Kavsquad, Kav Est1999, Greg Kav (YouTube). Her life demonstrates a new spiritual paradigm of a strength that invigorates instead of exhausts.

The process of releasing emotions in a safe space and place is crucial. Loss of a loved one either through a disagreement or through dying, transitioning, passing, any type of grief, grieving over the loss of a job, loss of a relationship, loss of a friendship, loss of age, loss of weight, loss of time, loss of a pet, loss of dreams, loss health, business loss, financial loss, loss of self (self-care, self-love, self-trust, self-respect, self-confidence, self-doubt, self-insecurities, self-worth, self -abandonment) – whatever the cause, grief requires a committed process to release.

Suppressing and oppressing feelings of grief is detrimental to holistic wealth and healing.

Life has uncertainties. This global pandemic may have bought to the surface your fear of uncertainty. Recognizing there has always been uncertainty, the nature of life is uncertainty. Inherent structure is uncertainty.

How comfortable you are with uncertainty will determine your level of freedom and tension release in your physicality.

The next moment is guaranteed to no one.

Life is precious, celebrating aliveness, celebrating each morning as I awake witness to the sun shining (even on the cloudy days) presence in the now moment, living each moment to your best it's fullest is key.

Manifest Your Best Life

I am grateful for my stories, life experiences, principles, lessons, methods, rituals, activations, ideas, ceremonies, habits, cultures in environments that demonstrate the characteristics to model.

Moving through the constructs of scarcity living, to sufficiency living, towards abundant living, I have been raised to new levels of awareness, personal fulfilment and success, drawing strength from the courage and resilience bestowed from the learnings of all seasons, experiences from mother nature, life lessons, ocean of abundance, the elements, the waterways and grounding earth under my feet and sand granules in between my toes.

One compassionate step at a time, the truth of our external nature can be revealed when dedicating, deliberately deciding, choosing experiences, explorations, education, evolution to expand you.

I welcome the same for you.

With a daily practice of self-awareness of your choice, intention, and the spiritual faculty, we can build our strength of choice to center our thoughts, emotions, physical body on the truth that God is good all the time. You have the choice to stay stubborn and loyal to your limiting beliefs, self-defeating choices, narrow or fixed viewpoints to an inner war, *or* you can choose abundant living which keeps you agile, relevant and alive.

The more heart-centered I become, the more I am deeply humbled by the auspicious reverence for life that no feeling is denied, condemned, or compared against another.

It is, I am, a preparation for greater expansion, recognizing greater blessings are on their way.

Once you start honoring yourself and your light, once compassion for the self is honored, living your highest values with a discernment, a holistic experiential internal external world opens, flood gates of soul-set alignment, access to a world so beautiful, so clean, so fresh, so spacious, so magical, and internal external divine unification with many moments that leave you bewildered, astonished, awe-filled, wonder-filled, taking your breath away.

I recommend an interactive exercise, one that has worked for me beautifully, as a guide. The suggestion is to look in the mirror **NAKED** to speak your real, raw, truth, no fantasy, no illusion, no delusion, just a real conversation with self.

Ask yourself with all masks off, all makeup cleaned, honestly and transparently?:

Are you living in a construct of scarcity? Do you recognize the signs of dis-stress in your life? Over-eating, over-stressing, over-doing? Is your mind cloudy, heart guarded, gut un-healthy? Are you operating from an untrained crocodile fight, flight or monkey mind or from your higher self?

Are you living in a construct of sufficiency? Are you dancing with awareness, developing gratitude practices that grounded in *self-mastery, self-responsibility, self-commitment, self-care, self-love, self-trust, self-guidance, self-clarity, self-valued, self-control?* Are you training your monkey mind, choosing to look at the stages and steps to manifestation with a focus on the self and an undercurrent of holistic wealth to move humanity forward, healing the "we"?

Are you living in a construct of abundance? Are you flour-ishing, radiant, moving forward with meaning and purpose, physically strong, vibrantly healthy, offerings of nourishing delicious fresh food waves of awareness, flowing in and out of equal value exchanges, an equanimity, an equilibrium, where yin/yang meet, harmonious, inner sense of tranquility? Are you focused on cultivating a higher vibration of light, healing the "us"?

I pray this chapter has sparked something in you to delve deeper and become *MORE* than a weekend interest reader, or a casual inquirer, or a self-help enthusiast, instead to choose partnership with a collective that has deliberately decided to be captains of their own ship, embarking and embracing next voyage with Awareness, Intention and Action. A voyage that when you know thy self, know your values, understand the art and science of pivoting and resilience with a willingness to commit to the manifestations that will materialize by design to handle and not of default or inertia to manage.

I pray that you deliberately decide to assist humanity in the transition. From whichever construct you are reading this, from whatever paradigm you are manifesting a deeper opportunity exists to help humanity and the collective. While it may seem you are merely one person on a singular journey, the patterns we face, the themes we face, and the conflicts we ultimately dissolve, resolve to evolve, the undercurrent of holistic wealth are the very gifts of shifting resistance to a renewed freedom, the frequency of abundance and living.

When you commit to healing thy self, you are committing to healing all.

"SEE YOURSELF LIVING IN ABUNDANCE AND YOU WILL ATTRACT IT. IT WORKS EVERY TIME WITH EVERY PERSON."

~ Bob Proctor

CHAPTER TEN

Abundance of my Trials and Success

By Lili Galera

How the Abundance in my Life has Shaped my Journey to Fulfillment

The abundant experiences I have witnessed in my life won't possibly fit in a chapter.

However, throughout my life, I have had time to experience so much and have been grateful to have realized that I'm still able to continue my journey while so many people's lives have been cut short. We have seen just in the last year that Covid has taken so many lives. I am blessed to be able to be part of this book and to continue being insightful and giving others light and direction. This insight fills me with gratitude in knowing that I've been blessed in my journey.

Why me? I've often thought.

For many years, I often thought that I might not reach the milestones of getting married, having children, or the fact of having achieved so much in my life so far. I would constantly question if I would make it to be 30 years of age, 40 years, or even 50. Yet, despite the years of worrying, time has proven that there are so many reasons for me to be alive and do so much more than I already have.

I believe that if we can appreciate how far we've all come in our lives, we can begin to see more clearly the abundance we've already been blessed with and manifest it to an even greater level.

It is with this thought that I would like to share how we can all be more abundant, especially despite the fears and worries that we might have regarding our future. In particular, I want to shed light on some special categories of abundance that I've struggled with and overcome:

The Abundance of Love, Entrepreneurship, Health, and Success

The relationships I have made throughout my journey have been extraordinary. Having an abundance of love to give and receive and sharing love is all-powerful and a massive part of my life. It's unconditional to give without receiving. Giving to oneself is necessary to move forward with loving others with abundance. Love can take shape in friendships, family, and with partners, and these have all shaped who I am today in abundance.

Business goals have been achieved in many aspects throughout my life. This is because I have taken an opportunity or an idea and somehow made it happen. You can do this, too. Have an idea, visualize it, and watch it transform.

Many people wish for wealth and to be successful but not always for the right reason, either due to having a sense of ambition or keeping up with status in life. However, we must realize there are many categories of success in one's life.

People often say to me that they would love to be successful and wealthy. I reply that no one can stand in the way of their success. You can achieve what you desire when you have plans, goals, and determination. When you have a purpose and strive for what you wish for, it can be achieved, resulting in a great sense of financial abundance.

Food was a constant source of abundance in my family growing up. I have often felt that there was more than enough food in most families, most of it going to waste. We have plenty of food and drink, perhaps too much. I remember preparing an abundance of food for a party or a picnic with my mother. The food was traditionally Italian focaccia and delicious homemade calzone. The preparation would take hours. Many people in Australia have so much food, and there are still so many starving people in other countries. It is important to step back, reflect on this issue, and consider what we do and how learn from this. Does food fulfil a gap of addiction or emptiness that we so often feel? Does it really assist us? I don't believe it does. In fact, it's the opposite. Because of this over-abundance, I have become obese and developed an eating disorder. The void or emptiness will be filled for a while for some, and then you're looking for more food to feel better if you are somewhat stressed or need comforting. It is a problem and we need to look at why we have become so gluttonous. We need to think of the health issues associated with the abundance of food and alcohol consumption and understand that as much abundance offers prosperity, it also requires moderation and discipline.

The abundance of Life: When you have achieved what you want, and you are content in your life and with what you are doing, you will feel a great satisfaction. This, for me, has been achieved mainly with challenging decision-making; making lifestyle choices of balancing a family and work CAN be achieved. Emotionally, it can be difficult to juggle both and try to maintain a social life as well. Things may not always go as we had hoped or planned. All we can do is have good intentions, do the best we can, and be the best version of ourselves.

There may be days, weeks, or months where we feel we can't get over the difficult challenges we are faced with. Some of these can be small and steady challenges that continue to escalate. Some may be huge challenges that we somehow do not know how we will overcome. But know that it's okay to feel overwhelmed.

We need to fall sometimes for us to be able to stand up again. Remember that children, we would fall and get up again. We didn't just sit on the ground and cry. Sometimes I remember getting up with the help of my siblings. There were times when I would fall and need to somehow get myself up onto a piece of furniture that was close by. We do what we can to get up off the floor, again and again, and conquer whatever is in our way. I like to tell myself I am not a failure if I do this. It is okay to put the idea on hold for a short period. Come back to your project at some other stage. Be kind and accepting towards yourself and move forward when you're ready. Pray on it; give it to the Lord, and manifest it. We may miss little things in a way that may not seem important, but they may be necessary for the full creativity of our ideas to come to fruition. Nurture yourself and know your limits. Small steps. That, for me, has been the key to success and abundance in my life as a whole.

Having an abundance of support and friendship is of great importance. There often seemed to be a lack of this in certain times of my life. I felt this isolation as a single parent. Being a divorcee was and still is often looked down upon. I felt guilt and shame to tell people what I was going through—being married to someone I loved and knowing that somehow regardless of seeing the red flags, I did nothing. Perhaps when I look back, not getting to know your partner well and making important decisions like marriage should not be decided at the lowest times of your life. That for me was when my mother had just passed away. We had only known one another for one year. There were too many unresolved issues in our relationship. It was a difficult time of my life being solo financially and emotionally. Some people may stay in a loveless marriage as they feel it's easier. But it is brave to leave and to be true to yourself, your partner, and children. With willpower and strength, I made the decision to keep going no matter what the consequences were till we parted and went our own ways.

These were times in my life where I didn't have an abundance of financial freedom. I was living on little wages working casual jobs, and had to raise two children under the age of five, which means I had to make significant lifestyle decisions. Some of these were going to caravan parks down south to Kiama with friends in a basic cabin. I would go to Paddy's Market to buy fruit and vegetables because they were cheap. I remember making sacrifices: no luxury holidays or spending on items that were not necessary.

I had decided to open my vulnerable side and let my children have insight into my life hoping that they would understand who I had become and why. This may also assist them in their daily lives and their future. To make them better understand that the difficult decisions I had to make were out of love for them. To love yourself and your children is selfless. It is not a weakness to open one's heart and be vulnerable at times.

Communication is very useful in all aspects of my life. Forgiveness is the most powerful gift to yourself. Carrying guilt or revenge for yourself or others can be painful and unhealthy.

 To love and be a good friend to others in my life has also had immense healing powers. Love is the most powerful of all abundances. It gives you the ability to heal and love yourself enough to keep yourself nurtured. It keeps you pure, divine, and helps you care for yourself. Positive energy is fuel for the soul, giving spiritual balance and growth. Choose to spend your valuable time with positive people in your life, and you will see a manifold of abundance take place.

With this, you should not forget to love yourself and to live your life with daily exercise and self-help books. Tune into your body and talk to yourself about discovering what your own needs might be. This is of utmost importance to be abundantly into yourself and in harmony with your body and soul. Nurture it before you can love and nurture others. How can you love others if you find faults and be hard on yourself?

I had often believed that it was the greatest gift for me to discover myself and who I really am. I did an abundance of soul searching. Being on my own for most of my life is and has been a really significant part of my journey of growth. I would lose myself in nature during long walks, being silent and still. I felt connected to the aboriginal spirits who respect and honor the sacred things and acknowledged that a long journey walking when you need to find the answer you're looking for was an abundance of self-love and care. I have loved others who have been close to me, and I have lost love through divorce and the death of people very close to me, including my parents. I have loved and not received love in return in relationships.

But one of the greatest lessons I have learned when it comes to abundance in relationships is that withholding love is selfish. Giving of yourself abundantly is being Godlike. It's a form of ascending to a higher dimension in the universe. This is one way that you can find more abundance in your life - through giving love to the people in your life.

Abundance in Health: How Food & Lifestyle has Shaped me

A second way we can find abundance in our lives is through something that we all enjoy: food.

Growing up with a European, middle-class background, food was abundant in my life, and my family was generous with their beverages and food that we would share with friends and guests.

Simply appreciating the blessing in disguise that food is can greatly increase your quality of life.

However, when it comes to food, it is important to remember that too much food taken in the wrong way can be a bad thing too. Overeating has many health implications, especially as it is the main contributor to heart disease and cancer. I speak from experience in my family and my own personal experience of going from obese to anorexic. Modify your eating intake. The best way to cultivate good health in life is to begin by cooking smaller portions of food. An abundance of food and drink can actually be detrimental to one's health if taken in the wrong way.

I have spoken to several obese people who have shared that they get depressed because of being overweight as they get very tired. I have sometimes experienced this at certain times of my life. Your overall lifestyle suffers when carrying excess weight.

Constantly dieting has been frustrating and challenging. My experience of going to various gymnasiums from a young age up into my current years has been rewarding, but also, there needs to be consistency. There needs to be a change in the way you approach your eating and exercise regime. It is important for us to all realize that while abundance gives us prosperity, it must also be balanced with discipline and moderation if we are to live healthy and happy lives.

Abundance in Achieving Business Goals

The third way I have seen abundance play a role in shaping my life is through entrepreneurship with hard work and discipline. Trusting my ideas and making them happen over different stages of my life. You can do this, too.

An abundance of work and businesses throughout my life has helped me build a future for myself and my kids and has allowed us to live a better lifestyle. Learning new skills, enrolling in courses, and constantly growing in your career improves one's life. This has been of utmost importance to me, regardless of where I was in life or what has happened.

Going to St Patrick's Girls High School at the Rocks Churchill and St. Patrick's Business College in The Rocks in Sydney was a vital part of my life. On our breaks or mass days, this is where I began my singing career. I loved to sing in the choir at church.

I achieved great things through hands-on learning, not just learning doing the theory, but doing both. I built on opportunities and jobs that I've had at different times of my life. One of these was recycling cutlery on a lathe for the airlines. Another was doing the maintenance work on a factory warehouse complex.

The ability to learn quickly in whatever industry or path I chose was to my advantage.

In particular, several business ventures have been incredibly fulfilling for me. I have had positions in a multitude of careers, some in the hospitality and travel industry, marketing, and customer service. I believe you can do anything you put your mind to. Immersing myself in different roles throughout my life has made me grow as a person and has made me who I am today, such as teaching Italian and reading to small children in Leichardt Library and being involved in Community of Christ church youth leadership role over the school holiday period. Volunteering in the local primary school my children were attending has also opened doors for me in other areas of my life.

My current role as a business owner of a rehearsal and recording studio has been a dream of mine for many years, stemming from my love of singing in the choir at school, music, dance. It is an extension of this love for music so that I could be with a network of like-minded musicians. I got to open a place for creative like-minded people where they could master their art.

Singing professionally has been one of the highlights of my life. I have been singing for over ten years as a freelance singer in the Sydney Entertainment Network.

One of my current projects is recording classic songs and posting them on social media platforms.

In short, I can say that the abundance of financial freedom and experiences in my life has come from my perseverance in pursuing opportunities.

More examples of this can be seen in the travel I've experienced over the years. This has been an integral part of my life and has helped me grow to become the person I am today. I went back to my parent's homeland, Italy. Other countries, like China, Malaysia, New Zealand, Vanuatu, The United States, England, Spain, France, and Fiji, made me who I am today. I have also traveled throughout Australia, making me appreciate this wonderful country I live in.

However, we must remember that while it is important to take opportunities, these opportunities don't come without their challenges. Overcome challenges, do not let the challenges overcome you.

Travelling was not easy for me at some stages of my life due to traumas in my past. I was once on a flight overseas that ran into bad weather (typhoon), and we had to stay in a hotel in Manila for several days. Being traumatized by this one particular incident meant I had to later overcome this specific fear of heights. This was a considerable challenge to overcome. It would be easier to convince oneself that I would not travel again because of fear. Seeking help from a hypnotherapist to assist me in overcoming my fear of flying was important.

From him, I learned that we are not birds, and we are not meant to fly. We are earth-bound, and as an earth sign, I certainly needed to be grounded.

If I wanted to see more of the world, I would need to seek therapy. A hypnotist and motivational tapes helped me to slowly manage my fear of heights. The fear can be so great that you think of nothing else - you become so numb, and you need to retrain your mind to imagine that you are not flying, that you are in a different place, like, for example, on a bus. I was able to overcome the fears, ultimately allowing me to travel again.

Good qualities of a business entrepreneur are to think outside the box, be a good leader, and connect well with people. Open your mind to ideas. Make them happen. Your intuition to do something or make a decision about anything can be very useful. Asking for advice from a professional can be helpful. Doing research for yourself on whatever you wish to achieve is the best way to approach your goal. Small steps and putting one foot forward have been some of my greatest freedoms.

I have also experienced freedom in abundance to listen to and trust my intuition. If you have a fear of failing, recognize this fear and learn to manage it. Improvise if necessary. Change things a little to accommodate your desires. Have you ever felt a push or a desire but were unsure what to do with it or what it meant? For example, it can be as simple as this: say you didn't have enough material for the long-sleeved dress you wanted for a special function. So instead of letting the fear paralyze you, you instead decide to make it yourself. It has to be completed in a few days. It can still be achieved by changing the sleeves' length, or the design, or the size of the outfit. For me, the example of the outfit is about how improving and adapting to one's opportunities and ideas is paramount. Going out of your comfort zone and taking a chance has always been the right thing for me to do. Seize your opportunity.

If you are looking for more abundance in your wealth, you can begin by taking the opportunities in front of you right now. You may have a voice of fear trying to sabotage you. It may be anxiety or a phobia, but you can always learn to manage these fears with enough persistence. Have the courage to move forward. Through this, you can achieve a greater abundance of wealth not only in your bank account but also in the richness of your life experience.

Abundance in Life: Connecting with Myself, Others, and Faith

Lastly, and perhaps most importantly, is the abundance that comes through your life experience of connecting with yourself, others, and your faith. Even if you had no one to love, no money to spend, or no food to eat, you can still find abundance through the connection that you have to yourself and the Higher Power of God. Through this connection, we can find an abundance of willpower and determination that defines our character and shapes who we truly are.

I remember when I would call upon God, my higher power, to give me an abundance of strength when I was traumatized many times throughout my life.

Looking back, I can see how every trial and tribulation helped shape my character into one of perseverance.

As the youngest of five, I was first taught the value of resilience and its abundance. Born in Australia, my family were European immigrants. Going to school when my first language is Italian was a great challenge. I was called a 'wog' at school (which is slang for foreigner.) This was offensive and hurtful. It wasn't easy to form an identity and understand who I really was. It was like I was living two lives. That still today is part of my confusion of my name(s) Liliana (the Italian) or Lilian (the English) name. I am both. Now, as an adult, I've chosen to be Lili.

Beginning a task at my studio that may have felt difficult to achieve and seeing the end result requires perseverance. I have planned my life around my career and relationships hoping that it would satisfy my needs and those of my family. I really think it has been the key to my success, and it has inspired me to never give up and to persevere in as many walks of life and all endeavors as I possibly can.

An abundance of spirituality with the spirit of God in my faith at school and in my household growing up made me feel loved and connected to the higher power of God. Even if I think I've been alone in my difficult times, I believe my angels were sending me love and light. That has been a powerful anchor, and it has helped me get through many problematic traumas throughout my life.

At the end of the day, we all have abundance all around us. It may take time for us to see it, but we can begin today by looking at what God has given us in our lives. From spending time with our loved ones and opening up to them to forgiving our enemies and those who hurt us. From taking opportunities that might scare us, like starting a new business or working through painful experiences we've had. From learning to appreciate the simple things in life like food or beverages to disciplining and moderating how we use such things. From being picked on at school to going through a difficult break up and raising children. Each and every one of these day-to-day experiences shape who we are, and just like in my journey, can lead us all to a fulfilling and abundant life.

"THREE KEYS TO MORE ABUNDANT LIVING: CARING ABOUT OTHERS, DARING FOR OTHERS, SHARING WITH OTHERS."

~ William A Ward

CHAPTER ELEVEN

Awakening to Abundance

By Travis Gray

Abundance is something that comes from inside of us; it's our birthright, it's something that we already have, we cannot earn it, and it cannot be taken away. Abundance starts with loving yourself and then giving your love away. If you try to gain self-love by giving to others that which you deny yourself, you will surely find an empty hole that will eat away at you each and every day.

This can be a surprisingly hard lesson to learn. It took me many years. I searched for abundance in everything but myself, and I never filled the empty feeling in my soul. This led me to a very dark place a decade ago, one from which I almost didn't return.

Physically, mentally, and emotionally bankrupt, empty and void of any hope left in my soul, I grabbed the gun from my nightstand, looked her straight in the eyes, then closed them and pulled the trigger! The soft click of the hammer slamming into the tiny little firing pin of that massive .45 caliber automatic was still radiating through my entire body like a shockwave as my eyes popped back open! Though our eyes only met for an instant, it seemed like an entire conversation flashed from her eyes to mine. What started out as shock, then turned into fear and then into disbelief, then instantly turned into the same disgust, disappointment, and disparity as was radiating from me. After twenty years together and the past ten years of anger, depression, isolation and addiction had brought us to a dark and scary place that both of us would barely survive!

Ten years later, as I sit here typing this right now, I can still connect with the pain and disparity flooding my heart and how desperately I just wanted it all to end. The past few years had been so hard that I really didn't have anything left inside of me. Then how my lungs surged back full of air from that first deep breath that I took as I came back into my body. For an instant, after I pulled the gun away from my head, I can remember just wanting to grab her and hold her and beg her to help me pull everything back together, but that's not what I did!

Instead, I jumped up from the bed, threw the gun across the room roared at her looking directly into her eyes as to pierce her soul with the same pain I felt that she was inflicting upon me. Neither one of us said another word, but I could hear her starting to cry and feel her heart breaking just a little bit more as I walked out of the bedroom door, through the house and out into the cold night air and disappeared as usual off to my own little private lair.

I sat there that night for several hours in that cold, dark and isolated room, completely numb and empty inside, almost like I was in a deep state meditation except for it was covered in a deep heartfelt, full body inner pain. I think I was in shock; it was like I had completely disconnected from my mind, body and spirit, and all that was left was my consciousness sitting and watching it all happen. I can still recall the way my thoughts started to phase back in and out as the room slowly heated up, and I came back to a sense of "being me". It felt similar to stories I've heard about out of body experiences except that I was watching everything through my body's eyes, but the body and eyes were not me. The best way I can describe it would be how the robots in some movies get damaged, and they start shutting down, blinking in and out trying to reboot/restart.

I wish I could say that this all happened in a moment of weakness or a fit of rage, but the truth is I can remember wishing for death and contemplating killing myself my entire life. Uncertainty, instability, neglect, isolation, abuse, betrayal and addictions throughout my childhood and teenage years had left me feeling fearful, insecure, unworthy, unlovable, untrustable, walled off and emotionally shut down. A lifetime of seeking stability, security, significance, happiness and abundance through possessions, relationships, money, power, dominance, prestige, and control had left me empty inside. I was 40 years old, lost, confused, unhappy, unhealthy and totally consumed by the life I had created and attached my identity to.

I couldn't buy enough toys, enough tools, enough safety, enough security, enough stuff and things. No matter how much someone else loved me, cared for me, and gave their heart way, I never felt valuable and worthy of other people's love; I always kept my heart tucked away. What you see coming out of yourself or others is what's inside, it's the abundance that you have to give away. I just didn't know that yet.

While the process I went through that night was life changing and affected me deeply in my soul, it took a little while to make sense of it all. Over time bits and pieces of what was going through my mind that night started coming back to me as I would sit in silence and just stare into nothing and once again go numb. I saw visions of my sons growing up without me and always wondering why I had decided to leave them, why didn't I love them enough to stay and what they had done wrong—seeing images of their lives that I had missed and the effects that their father killing himself would have on them long term. I saw my wife fall apart and blame herself and never recover from what she saw. I saw my family members crying and hurting for not being there for me and thinking there was something they could/should have done. Thoughts of how everyone who knew me would be affected by what I had done and the message it would send out to them. Thoughts of the reality of all kinds of possible outcomes of my actions started showing up for me all the time.

Things got a lot worse before they got better and there were several more times shortly after that that I sat there dying inside, crying alone and holding that gun. Something happened to me that night, though, and for the first time in my life, I started to realize that I truly wanted to live. I started seeing the beauty of my life, appreciating every moment and feeling so grateful for the miracle that I was still here. A deep inner fire had started burning inside of me, and it was starting to grow. The anger, pain, resentment, guilt, shame and regret was being interrupted by moments of peace, joy, tolerance, acceptance, forgiveness and the desire to die was slowly fading away. It took the reality of killing myself to finally find my desire to live.

That little voice still checks in on me now and then, but our relationship is much different these days. I used to sit and think about how much I would like to be free from this life, how it's just too hard, it's just not worth it, I don't have the strength to face another day and how much better this world would be if I were gone. I truly believed that killing myself would free me and let me just disappear, cease to exist, poof, it all just stops, and I would be gone! I used to sit and think about how wonderful it would be and entertain different ways of how I could do it—sometimes doing it in a manner that would hurt others and make them pay for hurting me or doing me wrong. Other times thinking I would do it somewhere that I would never be found. Making it look like an accident or driving off of a bridge or slamming into a bridge column or concrete wall.

Nowadays, when it shows up, I laugh at it, talk to it, ask it questions, smile at it, say a prayer of gratitude and appreciation for it reminding me of the pain and suffering that I used to create for myself with it and then lovingly let it go. I literally use the thought of killing myself to pause for a moment, breathe, meditate, open my heart space, bask in the warmth of the love I have found for myself and think of all the amazing moments I have had throughout my life and how life just keeps getting better and better every single day. I wouldn't say that I am happy that it still shows up sometimes, but I can say that I have found a loving and peaceful place for it in my heart, and I am glad to see it when it comes as it reminds me to stop to take a deeper look at myself and congratulate myself for how far I have come.

Sitting here ten years later at 50 years old after many painful years of searching, learning, discovering, challenging myself and exploring the depths of my soul, I have learned many things about myself and discovered how to create a life of purpose, passion and abundance that I could never have found on my own. I am honored and grateful to be able to be here now and share with you some of the lessons I have learned. Life is clearly a journey, not a destination. We are the authors of our lives. You cannot give away what you do not have; abundance is something we create from inside of ourselves, and it's available to everyone.

For those of you who are still entertaining the thoughts of how killing yourself is a solution to your problems, I pray that you can use my story to make the same shift that I was blessed with and give yourself permission to set it aside, take it off the table as a possibility, lovingly embrace it and allow it to fill your heart and fuel your flame. It all starts by making a committed decision that you will love and forgive yourself no matter what you've done and no matter what you continue to do. You can still work on growing and healing yourself while you love and embrace yourself for who you are, where you are at and where you are going to be. Make a commitment to yourself that you are valuable and worthy to yourself and that no one or nothing can ever take that away. Yes, there's a lot more to the process of actually feeling this truth in your heart but making a mental decision to love yourself and that you will choose to live is the first step in this journey.

Life's a journey, not a destination, is a simple statement that now resonates deep inside of me and speaks to my soul. I spent a large part of my life trying to reach a point at which I could be happy, peaceful, joyful, content, feel safe and secure, finally let my guard down, relax and be free. Now I know that this is only available in the present moment, and I can never reach a point that this will magically become true. I make this my reality for myself in every moment by accepting everything that is happening for what it is and not what I wish for it to be. Watching my inner state of being and separating myself and my value from other people, possessions or whatever is happening outside of me. Once I took suicide off the table, it forced me to look for other possibilities that were unavailable to me before.

What were once thoughts of giving up and getting out of here or drinking and drugging myself numb are now thoughts of curiosity and searching for the possibilities that each situation is opening up for me. What used to generate fear, anger, uncertainty, insecurity, guilt, shame, regret and a host of other dissatisfying and unpleasant feelings now fill my heart with hope and inspiration, knowing that I have the power to decide what it all means to me and that everything is happening for me and not to me and that I live in an abundant and benevolent Universe that is conspiring to give me whatever I truly wish to receive. I have made an agreement with myself to always choose happiness over sadness, and I have created a sacred space inside of myself that I can retreat to and find grace, love and forgiveness for everything that happens and everything I do.

I have decided to embrace and love everything about my past as it was all necessary in crafting and shaping the person that I am today. I have learned how to let go of my judgements, resentments, regrets, anger, and overall resistance to what I feel about the events of my past. I am now able to embrace almost everything that is happening and maintain my state of inner peace or quickly disconnect from pain, suffering, dissatisfaction, or thoughts that do not uplift, inspire, or motivate me. I have conditioned myself to use every thought or feeling of unpleasantness to trigger myself to stop for a moment, breathe and look for the lesson or blessing that this moment has available for me. Seeing life as a miracle and wonderful journey of experiences, discoveries, and endless abundance of possibilities has allowed me to look towards the future with excitement and curiosity instead of fear and uncertainty of the unknown.

By taking ownership and responsibility for everything that is happening and whatever results that I am producing, I now have the power to choose the meanings I am making and where I focus my mind and my energy. I used to look at life like I was just a player in the game, and I had to pick and choose from whatever life decided to make available to me. Now I see how I am not just a player; I am the author of my life, and I have the gift of creating and manifesting anything that I believe is possible for me. Stepping into the full understanding and reality of the true abundance and prosperity that is available to each and every one of us is still unfolding and growing inside of me. I still have much to learn and discover about this reality, but I have already learned and experienced so much that I know with all certainty that I can focus my energy and create whatever I choose to create.

I have learned many tools, techniques, strategies, processes, frameworks, and methodologies that I have tried, tested, adopted, discarded, and committed to fully implement into my life. The concept of, we don't find ourselves, we create ourselves has been very frustrating, confusing, painful and yet a wonderful, magical, and rewarding journey at the same time. I am working on an entire book dedicated to laying out in detail the step-by-step process that I have learned to define the life you wish to have and how to go about creating it. I wish I could say that I created it, but the reality of the "secret to life" is not really a secret at all. This information has been taught by many different philosophers, religions, teachers, gurus, kings and hustlers, players, and con artists a like, for thousands of years. It's way too much to cover in this one chapter, but I will share some of the details along the way.

The first step in creating a life of your own design, actually writing out your life story, is to suspend your attachment to the current story that you have about who you are and/or what has happened to you throughout your life. There are many different meanings and perspectives that we have available to choose from for everything about ourselves and everything that has ever happened to us. We have the choice to decide how we choose to define ourselves, others, and the events from our past, present, and future. This may be hard for some of us to understand and even harder to fully surrender to. I know it took me years to fully accept it, and I am still growing and learning how to apply it consistently and use it in my daily life. The basic concept here is to take ownership over the meanings that we are creating or have created around the events of our lives. You are the author of your life; you can write out your stories however you see fit to find value, education, motivation, inspiration, peace, forgiveness, acceptance, or any other reality you wish to create.

I'm not suggesting that you lie to yourself or use some form of trickery or diversion of the truth. I'm talking about taking an objective and non-judgmental look at your stories and ask yourself does this story benefit me and move me in a direction that I wish to go? Does this story add value to your life or is it a cancer eating away at your soul? Does your story cause anger, resentment, pain, disparity, guilt, shame, regret, or anything else that does not allow you to move forward and let it go? Does your current story benefit you in any way that provides some use or value in your life? If you cannot find value in your story as it is, then find another perspective or meaning that you could choose to make from it that will benefit you and take you in the direction you want to go.

That's right, rewrite your story and find a way to love it, embrace it, forgive everything about it and then use that new story as a tool to fill yourself with love, acceptance, forgiveness, grace, peace, joy or any other emotion you wish to create. Every time that old emotion shows up, dragging that same old defeated story up, acknowledge the old story, agree that the old story was whatever it was and made you feel however it made you feel and then pray over that old story by telling it thank you for showing up and reminding you how far you have come and how blessed you are for moving on from that story—as you turn your focus and energy towards the new story. This process has completely changed the way I look at everything from my past; I have been doing this for many years now. Most of the time, I can simply sit and love myself through any memory that shows up now. I don't even have to rewrite them to love them for what they were. Simply doing this repeatedly with your stories will literally rewire your mind to automatically look for the silver linings or the rainbows that always show up along with every storm.

Now, with all of that being said, if you don't have 40 years of baggage to unpack or garbage to sift through, you may be able to skip that step altogether. I do, however, suggest that you make a mental note of it, put it away in your toolbox but do not completely discard it or you may find yourself needing it in 20 years!

So, another part of being the author of your life in the present or the future is to actually take the time and energy to journal, write it out, talk it out in a mirror, record on audio/video or whatever else you can think of that will work for you. I highly recommend doing something other than just sitting and thinking about it, though. If sitting and thinking is all your willing to do, I suggest laying down, getting comfortable in a chair, sitting out in nature, by some water, or whatever it is that brings you peace and calmness and allows you to channel and focus your energy. It always helps me to get into a physical state before I work on my dreams. When I am rested, energized, focused and have created time and mental space to dream and explore my options and possibilities, I always come up with much better ideas than I do just sitting around at some random part of my day.

Focus your mind on looking at your goal, desire, situation....from a perspective of, if you were the author of your life, and you could simply write it out into the exact image that you wanted for yourself, what would that image be? If you had a wish, a magic wand, a genie in a bottle, infinite intelligence, God, Jesus, Buddha, the Universal cosmic energy field....what would your ideal, perfect outcome be? If you could have anything you wanted, what would it look like for you? If you're not really sure exactly what it would look like or you are open to many different possibilities, that's okay too. You can write out multiple stories, have fun with it, challenge your beliefs, comfort zone, or maybe make a connection to a book or movie that you love or anything that inspires you. The base objective here is to get the mind open to different possibilities or locking into the exact outcome you wish to create both and/or either of these has value and will aid in moving you forward or in the direction of your dreams.

Once you get clear on what you want or what is possible for you to achieve, then you start reverse engineering your vision into the first, smallest, easiest thing you can do right now to start moving yourself in that direction. Typically, I will do a who, what, why, when and how process on my item and create a clear vision sheet that describes in simple detail who I need to be, what does it look like, why is it important to me, when I wish to obtain it and lastly how will I go about getting it. How is the least important part of this process; the how is typically the one thing you will not know exactly what to do. You may have to learn something new, develop a habit, gain a skill, let go of a limiting belief, trial and error, test and measure…These answers are easier to discover working with a partner/coach who is focused on helping you discover the answers that you believe will work for you.

Once you get clear on what you are trying to do and how you are going to do it, write it up and review it regularly. Get into state, emotionally connect with it, visualize yourself having it, believe that it is possible, know that you are the author of your life. You can manifest things into existence through the power of your heart and mind. There are some very detailed processes out there for doing different versions of this and many books written about the power of the mind. I may be biased, but I think the book I haven't finished yet will be the best one to buy!

The fact that you cannot give away what you do not have was tough for me to wrap my head around. I mean, it made perfect sense, and I understood the concept, but what do I do? How do I generate something inside of myself that doesn't currently exist? Let me use the example that you cannot give love to others if you do not love yourself first. I mean, what exactly does loving yourself even mean in the first place. What does that look like? How do I love myself, where do I start, how do I measure this, track this or even know for sure that it's true? Those are all good questions and ones that you should be asking too. For me, it was pretty easy once I started digging into it all. I mean, I put what I believed to be a loaded gun to my head and pulled the damn trigger! That's a pretty clear sign that there are some self-love issues going on inside of there.

So, what did I do? Again, I started by taking suicide off the table as an option for solving my problems. Over the years of growing, learning, discovering and trial and error, I finally got completely onboard with the mind, body and spirit integration process and then very rapidly started seeing results. I can honestly say today that I truly love and appreciate myself, and I am proud to be me for the first time in my life. I will say that my motivation level has been affected, and I no longer care to attach my self-worth to success or external accomplishments anymore. I will also gladly walk away from opportunities and relationships that cause me dissatisfaction or others who are unwilling or unable to honor my boundaries or treat me how I ask to be treated. There are definitely some shifts of reality that I have had to adopt and habits I have had to create, but so far, I'm pretty satisfied with the results most of the time.

What is the mind, body and spirit integration process? It's where you take ownership and responsibility for defining/deciding who you are in those three areas and creating a system of managing yourself from three different perspectives which makes you stronger as a whole person. For me, it wound up being the answer to my self-worth and lack of self-love, among other things. I've found this to be true with pretty much everyone I have coached with or worked through the process also. Most of us have at least one area of our life that has been neglected, compromised or underserved to the point that it's affecting the way that we see ourselves.

The mind is where you look at/define/work on your beliefs, focus, meanings you're creating, thoughts that you are having, rules that you have for different areas of your life. Simply get a clear understanding of what's benefiting you and what's not. What you wish to change, grow, protect, acknowledge, eliminate, evaluate, learn, experience or whatever shows up for you throughout the process of discovery, it's different for everybody. We're really looking at what you believe is possible for you, what you are currently focusing on and making sure that you are actually paying attention to the things that are most important to you instead of the ones that are making the most noise.

The body is where we look at your physical body's health, fitness, physical state, diet, sleeping habits, addictions, illnesses, workload, self-image, the relationship between your body and mind, what you think about your body. This can be very different for different people also. For me, it was a little bit of all of those and more.

I have been clean from my drug of choice for nine years now. I have lost 60lbs and kept it off for eight years. I rarely eat snacks or drink sodas anymore. I exercise regularly, meditate, and have other self-loving body rituals that I do regularly. I have given myself grace for being imperfect to my vision of perfection. I love myself for who I am and continue to work each day at changing the things I can change and accepting the things that I cannot or do not feel like doing the work required to change. I would love to look like the Rock, but I'm not willing to put in that level of sacrifice and dedication that's required to make that a reality. I love myself for being honest about it, and when I look at my skinny legs, I smile at them tell them thank you for carrying me around all these years and never letting me down.

The spirit can get a little trickier for some people because we have different definitions around exactly what the word means. I use it in the context of our inner emotional state, connectedness to those around us, connectedness to the world around us and things of that nature. I don't make these definitions for other people, though. Instead, I simply ask them questions and help them clearly define what it means to them. Finally, we look at how all three of these areas interact with each other, effect each other, and look at how to integrate these areas to get you the results that you wish to create. Once I went through this process and made some changes in my behaviors, my beliefs, and my rituals, my level of self-worth, acceptance, forgiveness, tolerance, and overall value for myself grew and grew and continues to grow and grow each day.

Now I have more and more energy for myself and have plenty of extra to give away! I discovered the truth behind you cannot give away what you do not have by increasing the value I have for myself and seeing that I had more to give away!

Abundance is what we have inside of us to give away. When we forgive ourselves and others, we all have more forgiveness to give away. When we love ourselves by connecting with and honoring our minds, bodies, and spirits, we have more of everything to give away. When we serve and give to others, it fills our hearts back up, and we end up gaining more than we gave away.   Abundance is an endless circle that just keeps on growing as we give and never goes away.

I tried to drown myself with drugs and alcohol, and still, there came another day. I even tried to kill myself, and the gun was out of bullets. No abundance for me there either. It took losing everything that mattered to me and disconnecting from everything I considered to be me to finally find myself and the abundance that was in me all the way.

This is an abundant Universe; there is excess of everything! "The circumstances don't make the man, they reveal him"... this saying really hits home with me. To me, it means that my behavior is a mirror of my soul. Love yourself and value yourself first, and then you will have all the abundance that you will ever need to share and give away! I hope that you found some value in this and thank you for contributing to *The Journey of Riches series,* and I wish you all the abundance and prosperity that you desire in each and every way!

"When you arise in the morning, think of what a precious privilege it is to be alive to breathe, to think, to enjoy, to love."

~ Marcus Aurelius

CHAPTER TWELVE

Red Box Overflowing with Abundance

By AJ Myers

~ ~ ~ ~ ~ ~ ~ ~ ~ ~ ~ ~ ~

Measuring the Worth of Abundance

Have you ever found yourself under the canopy of a dark indigo sky, the whispering of leaves moved by the breeze and cicadas your only companions, a myriad of stars suspended above, and you search among them for your favorite constellation as you contemplate the state of your abundance?

This is me. I have a fascination with the night sky. Mighty Orion, bow stretched, facing Taurus: red eye flashing. But it is Libra, balancing the scales of justice, where my gaze lingers. Yes, justice, but I see more. I envision scales overflowing with gold coins on one side and sand on the other measuring the worth of abundance.

"Live as if you own the world," Mom would say to me when I would sigh for the desire of something just out of my reach. She had all these momisms to help us get through life's ups and downs. My parents walked their talk. "Just because you lose everything, doesn't mean you have to walk around with your tail tucked between your legs and look as if someone kicked you in the backside." I would hug my mom and plant one of my childish kisses on her check.

My parents lost pretty much everything, and I mean wealth, vehicles, home, and their ties to friends and family. Despite the downturn in financial lifestyle, Dad always had a box of chocolates for me. "Always make room for the little pleasures in life that you enjoy, Annie. It will never get so bad that you shouldn't spend a few pennies on sweets. Chocolates are for Kings and Queens, and you, little Princess, deserve the finest." I admit, some tears are rolling down my cheek as the curtains are pulled back on my memories. Dad loved to call me 'Annie Get Your Gun' because he said I had so much gunfire in me.

I stopped counting the times I seemed to be robbed of one thing or another. In July 2020, I was unexpectedly released from employment during COVID-19, over the phone, before the day had even begun. Like Libra, I stood and held my hands out, looking at one, then the other, balancing the scales of abundance. Once full, then suddenly empty. What happened? Like many of us, I found myself spiraling down a seemingly endless rabbit hole that I had visited too often for my liking when I felt betrayed. The various warrens and offshoots led to labyrinths within my convoluted and tortured emotions and mind to who knows where. It begins with shock and unbelief, quickly transitioning to anger and an internal dialogue of, "How could they? Why me?", or "Why is this the happening to me?" Then, because I can't direct my frustration on those I want to blame, I unintentionally lash out at my loved ones closest to me, those who will love me no matter what. Because the gaping wound created by the sense of what I lost is a portal allowing all I had worked so hard to attain to rush out, I then stand under the sky yelling…at God.

"If you love me, why are You doing this to me? How can You let this happen? What am I to do now?" and the tirade goes on long into the night. Voice hoarse, morose, depression begins to take a hold and settle into my belly. Some like to binge eat, turn to drugs or strong drink, others starve. Some, like me, become frantic robots. "Don't talk to me! I'm too busy," and we push people away. We become workaholics. The funny thing is, I didn't learn this from my parents.

It was through watching my Mother become other people's housemaid that I determined that would never happen to me. Ha! I learned, what you focus on is what you manifest: positive or negative. I was so focused on what *wasn't* going to happen, I didn't realize how I was setting up my future.

~ ~ ~ ~ ~ ~ ~ ~ ~ ~ ~ ~ ~

Fire!

"You need to come now, as there has been a small fire in your office." 6:05 AM. We had just come into town to watch our oldest son play in his college football playoff game. Not taking time to dress, my husband and I threw on shoes and grabbed coats to coverup our PJs.

"Small fire?" You have got to be kidding! Where an office building once stood, only rubble could be seen. 6:28 AM showed on the face of my wristwatch (cellphones weren't quite the thing then). I don't recall how long I stood there before TV news cameras and microphones were shoved in my face.

"Please, just go away! Can't you see I have lost everything?" I think I pleaded with these persistent people wanting to make the 7:00 o'clock AM breaking news. I was thankful for the protective barrier immediately created between the cacophony of news people, gawkers, and me. My 6'3 husband, son scheduled to play in his football game who stood 6'3, and our youngest at 6' were among my guard. My 4'11" frame seemed to shrink even smaller.

Our oldest son, cellphone in hand, began to punch in some numbers. "Who are you calling?"

"I'm calling my Coach, Dad. I need to be here with you and Mom," he earnestly responded without hesitation.

Have you ever had an epiphany so powerful that it knocks you to the ground? I mean like a bolt of lightning striking you... bam... right on the top of your head-- epiphany? There I was in a state of shock of what I had lost, my mind reeling with the millions of dollars I was potentially losing. And..., here was my son, fully aware of what was most important, most valuable on the day he should have been with his teammates readying for the playoff game, only hours away from kickoff. Suddenly, it seemed an airplane was flying overhead trailing a commercial in large bold type, "Abundance!" Was it mocking me? My mother's words echoed in my mind: "Just because you lose everything, doesn't mean you have to walk around with your tail tucked between your legs and look as if someone kicked you in the backside."

Numb, my life was rewinding at 10x speed, then playing forward in slow-mo as if I was having a near death experience. *I was a child again. Wonderful smells of warm baked goods consisting of chocolate, mint, and sugary icing wafting through the air and filling up my senses as my Mother was singing in her angelic soprano. Spatula in one hand and the decorating icing tube in the other to place the last rosette on a cake. There was no particular reason or special occasion; that's just what she loved to do for us. A little girl of five, I danced around, pretending I was Natalia Makarova, or imitating Esther Williams in one of her fabulous Hollywood extravaganzas. Fast forward, we were giggling and running in and out of the ocean's foamy white waves. Our lips blue from the cold and skin broken out in goose bumps. "No, we're not cold," we all chimed out unconvincingly to our Mom and Dad.*

The movie reel advanced... *"Me? Why would the King of Thailand want to present me with a gift?"* I had been singled out for this special, rare honor while I lived in Thailand... *"What a privilege, your highness, to be able to congratulate you and Princess Diana on your blessed union," I said, curtsying low on the side of the long, desolate road, on my way to Melbourne from Sydney, Australia, on a motorbike.* The movie kept playing, highlighting the overflowing areas of abundance I had experienced in my life in a compact version until it stopped at the point I was standing in front of my son.

The acrid smell of fire filled my nostrils. The blaring fire engines, police cars, and other first responders finally came to a halt, providing blessed relief. My mind was still having difficulty taking in the images of the twisted building structure, caved in roof, office furniture, computers, file cabinet, and everything one would expect of find in a thriving office. My personal office had been decorated in antiques and Shaker furniture, with special bound editions of Shakespeare, Audubon, Cassell, and the like. Original paintings had graced the walls gifted to me by my Mother and Father. All ruined.

"Watch out!" I shouted in horror; the metal struts melting away from the massive air-conditioning unit directly overhead a fireman. Crash! The unit just barely missed one of his feet as he quickly jumped back.

I realized in that split second that I had gotten it all wrong. I understood what my parents had attempted to teach me by them simply living their talk. How had my son got it right and I hadn't? How could he have understood that abundance is about so much more than money? He had never met my Mother and only met my Father a couple of times.

Although I shed no tears, both my sons cried that day. They cried for me because they had seen the many hours their Father and I had spent at the office and at home to work and build up a multi-million-dollar business. How many times had my husband called and insisted I come home because it was 2:00 AM and I was still working at the office to ensure our clients received their reports? How often did the employees come in the following day to find my husband and I had never gone home and in fact had been at the office for three or four days non-stop, working? I lost count of the number of times I had to ask my youngest son to forgive me because he was left sitting at school long after the time when I should have picked him up. Thankfully, we came to an amicable agreement. We rotated between trusted employees to pick him up and bring him to my office where he could do his homework. Then, for a few hours, I paid him to help with clerical duties. Bless his heart, my son wrote his BA thesis on *Best Employee Retention Practices* based on what he observed at my company. We worked hard so we could play hard.

Saturday of Labor Day weekend, 2001, is when the fire at the office occurred. We got through that with a lot of help from abundant sources we never expected. For three or four days, the fire brigade showed up. Each day, they fed us breakfast and lunch as my husband, our key employees and I set up tables on the blacktop to sift through the ashes and begin the arduous process of inventorying whatever we could find into piles of what could be salvaged, what was confidential and had to be shredded, and what was trash. For about a week, firemen and friends assisted us. Even our son's college and high school football buddies helped when they could.

We learned a hard lesson: Insurance companies are not in the business to give you help. At the time, we were paying close to $17,000 per month just in insurance premiums. Where were they and the policy coverages when we needed them? Do you know what a "no see 'em" is? These itty-bitty insects are aptly named because you cannot see them. I now refer to insurance companies as "no see 'ems", too-- nowhere to be found when you need them. Late a few days on paying that premium and they come crawling out of the woodwork like termites. Anyway, I am digressing...

We scheduled rotating shifts beginning at 5:00 AM and ending at 3:00 AM, seven days a week, with office space setup in just about every area of our home that you could find a place to sit. This meant we had to displace our children and appeal to friends to take our children in their homes during this emergency period. How about that for infringing upon friendships? Remember, this was over a Labor Day holiday weekend. Special truncated phonelines had to be laid in, the Fire Marshal had to come and approve extra power lines and increased circuit amperage for computers and employees being in our home, special permits for parking, business use, increased water and sewer usage had to be acquired, etc. We had to find businesses that were open and willing to deliver high-powered office equipment and furniture, IT personnel to setup networks and all that entailed and, we had to be functional, operational, as if nothing had ever happened, by 7:00 AM the very next business day. Because we worked in healthcare, patients did not stop being ill, cancer didn't stop eating away at people, accidents did not disappear, and doctors didn't all just simply go on vacation. Abundance?

Yes, we learned the Abundance of loyalty, duty, and determination. Two of our key employees had spouses bring overnight bags so they could sleep over at our home. So many members of our team stayed and worked during those difficult circumstances for a period of about four months until new office space was found. Together, we made it work, and not one of all the clients and thousands of patients knew the tragedy and pain of what we had undergone and the continuing conditions we had to operate within, except for one…, our newly acquired client, the largest. Because the Director of Ancillary Services of a large hospital lived in the same area that I did, when she and her daughter were going out for breakfast the day of the fire, the little girl asked, "Mom! Isn't that the building where the company is that works with you?" Otherwise, even they would never have known because of the extraordinary measures we took to ensure preservation of all our client and patient records; they were triple backed up at multiple offsite locations. Thank heaven for that precaution we paid bookoo bucks (a lot) to put into place. Before you breathe a sigh of relief though, remember the old adage, life slings its darts in threes. This was number two. My dear Father had passed away just a few months earlier while we were on vacation during the summer.

We had taken our children across the States for their summer school break when one of my sisters called out of the blue. "You need to get to the hospital as soon as you possibly can. The physician said to 'urgently round up the family'." We were more than 500 miles away from the nearest airport. Thankfully, I always pack my US Passport, a habit from the days of living out of a suitcase when I was single. Airline tickets for my little Shi-a-poo dog and I purchased, I arrived in time. The hospice nurse said Dad hadn't eaten, spoken, or opened his eyes in three days. As I held his hand and leaned in, I named each of the 12 children he had adopted, recounting

the abundance he and Mom had sowed into us. I told him it
was okay to let us go to be with Mom again. I kissed him
'goodbye'.

~ ~ ~ ~ ~ ~ ~ ~ ~ ~ ~ ~ ~

Under Attack

Exactly seven days after that fateful call informing us there
was a 'small fire,' one of the employees walked into our bedroom. My husband and I had just laid down from working approximately 40 hours without any sleep. "I'm sorry to barge in
but you weren't answering. Your son is on the phone and it's
urgent."

"Okay. Thank you," I said. "I'll take it in here. Please shut the
door." I picked up the phone, and, before I could say anything,
my son told me to turn on the TV. "But we just laid down.
May I call you back?"

"Mom, you don't understand! We are under attack! A terrorist
has flown into one of the Twin Towers!"

"Are you kidding me? Please, I am too exhausted…"

Highly agitated, he barked, "Mom… just turn it on. Wake Dad
up!"

9/11. Disbelief as the image filled the TV screen of a plane
crashing into the second Twin Tower.

"God, NO!" I remember screaming, and I do not take the
Lord's Name in vain. "NO! This can't be happening!" I
dropped the phone.

"What is it?" my husband asked groggily. I just pointed at the television. Then, suddenly I remembered my son was on the phone.

"When did this happen?" I asked him. He told me he had been getting ready to go to the gym. "Do you need me to drive home?" he asked, willing to drop everything and leave college to come home. "No, Son... I love you. Are there any protests going on at the campus? Have fights broken out?" He assured me he was okay.

Without a thought of how I looked, I ran out of the bedroom and yelled to the employees to turn on the large screen TV. We all watched in horror and cried. The day continued in fear as we prayed and watched part of the US Pentagon cave in. We gasped and broke down when the highjacked Flight 93 crashed in Pennsylvania. How? Why? Aren't we the Land of Freedom? Isn't America the Beacon of Hope and Light? Doesn't America embody the very essence of Abundant Living?

As owner of the company, I felt it was my duty to rally the employees and do all that was possible to instill hope. Changing, I threw on some clothes. Asking everyone to come outside with me, I suggested we gather in a circle around the flagpole erected in my front yard, hailing the American stars and stripes.

"We are under attack like never before in our lifetime. Our values, morals, and principles are being attacked. Our right to religious freedom; to gather and worship openly as we so desire, our freedom of speech, and our very right to live free, to work and live the American Dream are under attack. I am asking if you will gather as one, under the American Flag that many have fought, bled, and died to defend, and pray with me. Pray for those who have died this day. Pray for the injured. Pray for those who have lost loved ones. Pray for businesses. Pray for the restructuring of this Nation, for our Leaders, for Wisdom from Above, for Leadership, for Protection against the enemy, for each of us, for our company as we continue to operate in my home, for strength and endurance during these trying times, for unity in our shared purpose, for kindness and forgiveness, and for patience for we know not what will come out of this day. Pray that our Land, our Country will be united in its cause to rid the enemy from within and from those that are without; to reestablish its protective borders so we may breathe free. Pray for peace around the world. Will you stand with me as we remember all that we must be thankful for?"

Not one walked away. All of us stood arm-in-arm. Cars slowed to wave at us and show their support. We then each went around the circle and shared what we were feeling and gave a statement of gratitude. We sang, "God Bless America," "Battle Cry of the Republic," and "Star-Spangled Banner," our country's national anthem. We all recited the Pledge of Allegiance. We stood there under the waving flag: those born in

America, white, American Indian, first generation Korean, Russian, Armenian, Romanian, Vietnamese, Chinese, African American, and we didn't see ethnic differences. We sang with one voice, in one language, for one country, united. We claimed America's Abundance of "Freedom, Liberty, and Justice for All".

But this isn't the end of my story.

~ ~ ~ ~ ~ ~ ~ ~ ~ ~ ~ ~ ~

Moving on Up to the Eastside

Eventually, we found a better and more plush office space to house the company and its employees. It was a fresh start, and the business grew to twice its original size. We had made it. Bank accounts, retirement, and stock portfolio all evidenced that we were living financially abundant.

A home takes on the character of its occupants and the oft repeated quote, "If only these walls could talk…" seemed to be fitting after our home was turned into an emergency office. The joy and peace of 'home' was gone, no matter what renovations we did. We needed to move.

"Oh, look at the yard and the space for gardening," I exclaimed. The pine green, ranch style house with white trim, peeking out amidst a parklike forest of stately cedars was my dream home. After ensuring our children could continue to attend their same high school, especially since our youngest son was Co-Captain of their State Championship football Team, we closed the home agreement. In less than 30-days from the day I walked on the expansive back deck, we had the home furnished and moved in.

Money was no object. This exclusive neighborhood boasted professional athletes, politicians, and Hollywood movie stars. We had moved up and into the upper Eastside and were living among the financially affluent.

Life was grand! My boys' high school football team were experiencing win after win, claiming seven State Championships to date that I am aware of. Both were Co-Captains, and I was a Team Mom. Our daughter was becoming successful performing American Sign Language on major concert stages at the age of 16 after nearly dropping out of school. We held season tickets to major league baseball and took the boys to national football games. My husband golfed at least four times a week that included rounds with Arnold Palmer, Johnny Miller, Susan Sanders, and other pros. Our golf membership allowed our children to hob nob with celebrities in between their scholastic and other athletic obligations. We secured one of the premier moorings for our yacht so we could watch fireworks over the water.

Summers were spent camping at the lake and traveling, while winters were spent snow skiing and on snowmobiles at various ski resorts. We were generous with our abundance. Our children's friends, our family, and our friends were brought on our trips: all expenses paid. I was active in Healing Ministry serving others while still managing to visit my ailing Father, paying for whatever he needed, always responding, "God has richly blessed us. Allow us to share our abundance," adding, "while we still have it." Why did I add that last bit?

~ ~ ~ ~ ~ ~ ~ ~ ~ ~ ~ ~ ~

New Meaning of Abundance

Impressive as our abundant lifestyle was and despite the growing business and new home, my insides had been crumbling. The physical, emotional, mental strain, and stress I had endured landed me in a place that took me several years to crawl out of. That statement that I always ended with, "… while we have it" finally manifested a few years after the devastating fire.

Health failing, my husband called 911. I was experiencing the symptoms of a heart attack. Goredforwomen.org cites that cardiovascular disease is the number one killer of women in America, with one in three deaths annually. Do the math. That is about one woman every minute! My business was healthcare. I was quite familiar working around physicians and being in medical facilities on a regular basis. That was the first time I consciously experienced such frenzy over me. I was on close watch for some time after that. I was concerned, but not as scared as my husband and children. That coupled with the serious run of auto accidents I had been a victim of, I was resigned to bed for the next three years.

Recognizing the need for help, I made a couple of bad missteps in hiring an Office Manager and Marketing Director. Seeing an opportunity in my vulnerable state, they conspired to get a foothold into the inner workings of my organization and take control of a company my husband and I had spent 12 years building with our blood, sweat, and tears. My husband's attention was focused on taking care of me. Employees I relied on were sloppy because I wasn't present to dot all the 'i's and cross the 't's. In the years I personally managed the operations, we received one patient complaint. One. Do you know how remarkable it is to maintain a stellar customer service rating of that caliber? In the 14th year, five complaints came in, and when I asked why, they all echoed pretty much the same thing. Then more began to come in. Something was wrong.

Long story short, I fired both the Office Manager and Marketing Director, but the poison had spread. Now the physicians were calling me directly for an explanation as to what was going on. There could only be a couple of explanations: Computer glitch or human error/theft. We found a combination of the two and addressed them both believing we had put out the fire. One of the doctor groups was down by more than a quarter million and I vowed to right the ship. I worked with the Programmer and IT personnel. After pouring over numerous tests and reports, I found a devastating anomaly, far worse than what I could have possibly imaged. This finding coincided just at about the same time my phone rang. Three years in bed, my company had been bleeding.

"AJ. Can you come to the office? I need to confess why the company is going under," she says at 7:30 AM on a Saturday when the office is closed. She knew the Medical Director was coming in to meet with me at 9:00 AM to get to the bottom of why his medical office was looking to close their radiology practice resulting from the poor performance provided by my company.

"What do you mean you need to confess? Confess to what?" I asked her, afraid I knew the answer based on what the reports had revealed.

"I have been lying to you all these months…" Without going into all of the ugly details, I immediately made a call to the Insurance Broker to enact the E&O insurance policy of three million per incident per employee for fraud, theft, etc. It was odd how I never could get through to her, or anyone else at the insurance agency. I shouldn't have been surprised given my experience during the fire claim. My next calls were to cash in my stocks and retirement policies at huge losses. I shifted over the bulk of my personal cash I could lay my hands on to the business operating account. By the time I met with the Medical Director, I was able to assure him that every penny owed to his medical facility and each physician, due to the lack of performance of my company, would be in his bank first thing the following Monday morning.

That was another evening I found myself gazing up at the night sky, searching for Libra. Did her scales hold an abundance of gold coins, or was the sand being weighed against lumps of coal? I stood alone and held my hands out, looking at one, then the other: once full, then suddenly empty. Again, I felt I had been betrayed.

Did I have to do this? No. I could easily have filed bankruptcy and gone on to live a financially secure, abundant lifestyle. But how abundant would my life truly have been? What example would I have set for my children?

One Christmas, not too long ago, completely broke, and mimicking my parents of years long gone when they had lost all their holdings, I looked at my fake Christmas tree. It wasn't the 10', full tree all decked out in Lenox and Waterford Crystal, and porcelain angels. No. It was just a cheap, fake tree I picked up on clearance with a few ornaments. Looking at my two sons, daughter-in-Law, and husband, I apologized for the lack of gifts because under the tree were only 4, 4"x4"x4" red cardboard boxes I had made for each of them. I had lost my mother years earlier, but her words of wisdom are still with me, "Just because you lose everything, doesn't mean you have to walk around with your tail tucked between your legs and look as if someone kicked you in the backside." Before handing the red cardboard boxes out, I asked if we could go around and say one thing we were grateful for about the person sitting to our left. I happened to be sitting to the left of my oldest son.

"Mom, of all the people I have encountered and know and that I have played with and against on the football field, you are the most courageous, toughest person I know. You have taught me to live with integrity. You are the one who taught me years ago that Abundance is not about money but about how we live with what we have and to how to love." Yeah…I broke down and cried.

Oh, and the red boxes, sitting under that little Christmas tree… those were prayer boxes containing prayers I had typed for every day of the year for each of them. I had no money for anything to buy. My heart, though, was full of Abundant prayers. God has allowed me to go through experiences in such a way to learn how to live overflowing Abundance in every area of my life and share this with the world.

Now, I look up at the night sky, and search until I find Libra. She is holding each prayer in one scale and gold coins of Abundance in the other.

"ABUNDANT LIVING IS REALIZING THAT LIFE IS A PRIVILEGE WHETHER IT'S ADHERING TO OUR SCRIPT OR NOT."

~ Craig D. Lounsbrough

Author Biographies

Belinda Foster

CHAPTER ONE

Belinda Foster believes abundant living is about experiences and the people you meet along the way. She has worked in the banking and finance industry for 35 years. She's been a radio show host, a Yahoo Contributing Writer, managed a famous blues-music musician, produced a music festival, was a music critic and wrote a monthly entertainment news column for a local publication. Belinda's been a certified personal fitness trainer, a bodybuilder, and has worked in holistic and natural health in nutrition and a quantum energy biotech industry as a national trainer.

Born in 1961, she grew up on the North Carolina coast in a small fishing community where she 'headed shrimp,' shucked oysters, cleaned crabs, and handed tobacco. She loves the beach and spends most of her time on the South Carolina coast and the rest of her time at her home near the NC mountains. Her favorite hobbies are kayaking, tennis, boating, golf and developing deep, long-term friendships. Justice, truth, and ser-vice are her calling, and she will take on any project in which she aligns as long as it is helping humanity and others and is of truth and value. Belinda's belief in God gives her the faith to take chances and live on the outer edges of expanding the never ending life of abundant living.

John Spender

CHAPTER TWO

John Spender is a 23-time International Best Selling co-author who didn't learn how to read and write at a basic level until he was ten years old. He has since traveled the world and started many businesses leading him to create the best-selling book series *A Journey Of Riches*. He is an Award Winning International Speaker and Movie Maker.

John worked as an international NLP trainer and has coached thousands of people from various backgrounds through all sorts of challenges. From the borderline homeless to very wealthy individuals, he has helped many people to get in touch with their truth to create a life on their terms.

John's search for answers to living a fulfilling life has taken him to work with Native American Indians in the Hills of San Diego, the forests of Madagascar, swimming with humpback whales in Tonga, exploring the Okavango Delta of Botswana and the Great Wall of China. He's traveled from Chile to Slovakia, Hungary to the Solomon Islands, the mountains of Italy and the streets of Mexico.

Everywhere his journey has taken him, John has discovered a hunger among people to find a new way to live, with a yearning for freedom of expression. His belief that everyone has a book in them was born.

He is now a writing coach, having worked with more than 300 authors from 40 different countries for the *A Journey of Riches* series http://ajourneyofriches.com/ and his publishing house, Motion Media International, has published 31 non-fiction titles to date.

John also co-wrote and produced the movie documentary *Adversity* starring Jack Canfield, Rev. Micheal Bernard Beckwith, Dr. John Demartini and many more, coming soon in 2020. Moreover, you can bet there will be a best-selling book to follow!

Abhinav Gupta

CHAPTER THREE

A bhinav Gupta is a Business Coach and helped many businesses in Australia and the Philippines, UK, and USA scale to six Figure Income per month. He lives in Melbourne; Australia loves to help people through his teaching others to be passionate about giving value to their clients.

Abhinav has run many successful businesses in the Telecommunication, Energy industry, worked as a corporate professional as Business Development Manager. He was introduced to a network marketing company aligned with his beliefs and values and committed to developing the skills necessary to become a top professional in that industry. In 2019, he was awarded a Top-ranking achiever in his company. Today, he is passionate about helping many others achieve their goals and inspiration either in traditional business or Network Marketing.

He is married to his wife, Poonam Aggarwal, with a child, Neil Gupta, born in 2012.

He migrated in 1990 to Australia with his parents Mr. Suresh K Gupta and Mrs. Sunita Gupta.

www.abhinavgupta.com.au
abhi235@hotmail.com
+61 449 873 127

Harmony Polo

CHAPTER FOUR

Harmony Polo, CEO, healer, musician

Harmony is a natural born healer, musician and businesswoman. She began her quest to deepen in the healing arts at the age of 33.

In this time, she uprooted her life as a celebrity hairstylist to the stars to explore eastern healing, philosophy and spirituality. She studied different healing modalities with teachers in Bali, Indonesia and India. Harmony has been working as a private life coach and healer for over ten years. This includes sound healing, Mantra singing, energy work, Deeksha, business coaching, life coaching, addiction and kundalini yoga.

With her international roots, two albums and a plethora of wisdom, she expanded her energy to open a new Harmonic Egg healing center in Naperville as a perfect way to upgrade and expand her healing roots. Harmony has also composed, produced and recorded healing mantras for the Harmonic Egg. Her ability to invoke presence within her angelic voice creates deeply healing and loving energy to assist in the healing journey with the Harmonic Egg.

Anastasia Gunawan

CHAPTER FIVE

As a millennial, Anastasia is passionate about sharing her discovery to authentic life and success with others. Anastasia is a scientist, educator and advocate for real food, brain health, and wellness. Anastasia has consulted with the government, academia, non-profits, and private organizations in large scale community health initiatives.

In 2020, she became a pandemic first responder and provided critical intelligence, technical assistance and research towards COVID-19 mitigation and operations. Anastasia's first-hand perspective in systemic global unrest and turmoil led her to seek answers to prevalent questions post pandemic society: What is the new normal?

Anastasia is also a big advocate in empowering small communities through outreach and education to achieve sustainable positive health impacts. Anastasia believes in empowering others by becoming the change she wants to see in the world. She is the founder of The Burnout Millennial – a grassroots online movement with a simple mission to end stress and burnout epidemic https://tbom.us and a co-author in the international best-selling book *A Journey of Riches, Liberate Your Struggles.*

She currently lives in Reno, NV, the USA, with her loving partner and enjoys hunting for wild hot springs throughout the Sierra Nevada.

Samuel Sykes II

CHAPTER SIX

Samuel Sykes II is a brilliant global executive business-man, international scientist, entrepreneur, mentor and ingenious solutionist. Mr. Sykes embraces the archetype of innovation, intelligent intuition and income generation!

For 14 years, Mr. Sykes was an award-winning international research and development expert for Kimberly Clark Corporation. Recognized by fellow scientists, engineers and patent attorneys, he garnered the designation of "Inventor" for patents filed and granted in the U.S. and other foreign countries: Australia, Canada, Europe, Brazil, Colombia, Argentina, Korea, Taiwan, Japan and Mexico.

Co-author of a book with Deepak Chopra, Dr. Wayne Dyer, Mark Victor Hansen, titled 'Wake Up & Live The Life You Love, Finding Your Passion,' which became a #4 Best Seller upon its first day of release.

Successful track record with several start-up companies where cutting edge concepts and marketing strategies have consistently been proven throughout his business career.

Samuel's greatest assets are his knowledge of people, extensive business relationships, and the ability to leverage those assets to turn vision and concepts into reality. Sykes motto "Words Impress people, but actions and results inspire."

Mr. Sykes enjoys spending time with his rescue dog "Maggie," quality time with family and friends, but most importantly, he loves becoming a better man each and every day while helping others!

In a world of unfulfilled promises, Samuel's solutions have arrived that carry a vision of the future and will forever change the way people and businesses think.

BeSecure within yourself.....within your finances.....within your LIFE.

Samuel Sykes II
besecureinformation@gmail.com
PO BOX 83
Greenville, WI 54942

Lanelle Martin

CHAPTER SEVEN

Dr. Lanelle Martin has earned her Ph.D. of Theology - Doctor of Divinity, while an entrepreneur, career woman, wife, and mother of two young boys. Her affinity for making connections led her to launch a successful business networking group in 2005 to serve its members today.

Meeting the fundamental needs of families and individuals became of great interest, prompting her to start an organization focused on quick, trusted remedies of personal help, emphasizing support for caregivers and Moms worldwide. Today, that organization is spreading into personalized loving communities of support one person at a time.

Dr. Lanelle's passion, initially known as "My Support Network," has transitioned into a significant calling with the growing and ever-changing needs surfacing in today's unique world. Now, "WeLink" is a personalized, loving support community led by a higher awareness of connection to others. Dr. Lanelle's calling makes her a Worldwide Community Connector.

Sam Frazer

CHAPTER EIGHT

S am Fraser has had 32 laps around the sun. From growing up in uncertainty, violence, and much confusion from society's way of being, he struggled to manifest his dream reality through his unconscious awareness from his conditioning that limited his belief systems in many areas of his life.

Four years ago, Sam had an awakening and transitioned from a stressed, lost soul working as a carpenter/builder contractor to now; new earth guide, intuitive mentor, healer, Channeler, multidimensional alchemist and 5D business owner where he and his team guide others throughout their awakening journey of rediscovery and empowerment for their unique soul-aligned purpose in life as way-showers for the safe and sacred evolution of humanity and mother earth's conscious rising.

Sam has had many struggles throughout his life and found much comfort in the thought of there being more the world and himself could offer. By losing himself within the party scene, taking all kinds of recreational drugs to fill the void of emptiness he felt every day, losing his business in a recession was a clear catalyst for him hitting rock bottom. Sam began searching for answers, and this was when he truly started his hero's journey to abundant living four years ago.

Catherine Kavadas

CHAPTER NINE

Catherine Kavadas resides in Sydney, Australia, with her family, childhood sweetheart of 26 years and their four cherubs, who are her proudest creative expressions of love, miracles, and joyous gifts to date and beyond.

Catherine graduated from university with a double degree in Bachelor of Commerce/Law (Majoring in Business). As a law practitioner for several years, she obtained her unrestricted practicing certificate before moving into the commercial space as a professional indemnity underwriter of an insurance company.

Her greatest honor, privilege, challenge and growth professionally is with Alex, her husband, who owns and runs a property repairs and maintenance business in a service-based industry. As the humanitarian arm of their business, Catherine is a passionate contributor, paying it forward to visionary and humanitarian projects aligned with their family values.

Catherine has been working with Ruth Posterino, visionary of Personal Leadership Academy.

If you want to further connect with Catherine, you can do so by emailing catherine@personalleadershipacademy.com.au or heading over and checking out the excellent resources on www.personalleadershipacademy.com.au, or called to contribute to

Go Fund me:- gf.me/u/zkcr5i Proceeds go towards 50 scholarships fueling a mission of integrity and wisdom to self, families, teams, communities, enhancing the lives of our good leaders who are prioritizing the education of self-mastery, which ripples to making a difference.

One of Catherine recent favorite quotes is *"All new life exists in this moment"* ~ Adam Markel

Lili Galera

CHAPTER TEN

L ili Galera resides in Sydney, NSW, Australia. She is a freelance singer and also manages a business in Music. Lili has been singing for over ten years in and around the Sydney music scene.

Her ethnic background is primarily of European descent.

Lili's primary career started as a secretary and worked in most areas of a corporate office. She has a background in Real Estate, Marketing, Management, Secretary, Teaching, Customer Service in Postal Services, Commonwealth Bank and Government careers such as Parliament House Receptionist to the Minister for Education.

Also, she has been self-employed in various industries. i.e., Airline Catering Dept. (recycling of cutlery). For Education. Adult Migrant Services, Music Board, Education Department, Hospitality Industry. Secretary and Stenographer to a Medical Surgeon.

Lili has successfully completed courses in Hospitality Supervision. Valuations Business and Real Estate. She has studied extensively over the years at Ryde College of TAFE, Granville TAFE and St. Patricks Business College, and TAFE NSW.

Travis Gray

CHAPTER ELEVEN

Travis Gray is an author, speaker, teacher, and rapid transformational CoachSultant focused on mind, body, spirit, purpose, and passion. He has his ICF certification in Human Potential and Emotional Intelligence, among many other personal and business-related accreditations and certifications. Travis is a 5th generation entrepreneur, and his primary focus is to assist Entrepreneurial Men ages 40-60 in navigating through life's challenges and creating lives of purpose, passion, and contribution.

Travis is now at the age of 50 and is the fourth of five children. He has two sons of his own, Joe, 20 and Cole, 17. Travis was born and raised in Arlington, Texas, where he resides today. He enjoys a happy, healthy, active life of adventure, travel, learning, exploring, and experiencing all that this life has to offer.

After narrowly surviving a dark 10-year bout with addiction, divorced after 18yrs of marriage, and a large part of his adult life devoted to seeking fulfillment and value from external sources, Travis is now passionately dedicated to serving others. He has spent the past ten years deep-diving into personal growth and exploring the depths of the human soul. Travis is currently working on several books sharing his unique perspective and lessons learned along the way. The best way to contact Travis is through his Facebook page at https://www.facebook.com/travis.gray.148/.

AJ Myers

CHAPTER TWELVE

A J Myers, God's Writing Warrior and artist is founder of Heart2Pen [https://www.facebook.com/groups/146556096836287]. She lives in the USA.

AJ was determined to help two billion others who find themselves in a place of hopelessness to claim their uniqueness: to be whole, healed, and to live in overflowing abundance when, unexpectedly, she became jobless, without medical insurance, while being sole caregiver to her terminally ill husband.

She watched her mother clean other people's filthy toilets while raising 12 adopted children after she and her father were swindled out of everything they had built up, and her health failed. She died early. Vowing that would not be her fate, AJ realized that through her inspired, written words and art these billions could find hope and healing.

AJ's pieces appeared in May Lux, Write & Shine, and CTC publications. Her story is in "Journey of Riches": 25th book,

"Abundant Living". AJ has/is collaborating on several projects, and book one of four of her novel series will soon be released.

"DOING WHAT YOU LOVE IS THE CORNERSTONE OF HAVING ABUNDANCE IN YOUR LIFE."

~ Wayne Dyer

Afterword

I hope you enjoyed the collection of heartfelt stories, wisdom and vulnerability shared. Storytelling is the oldest form of communication, and I hope you feel inspired to take a step toward living a fulfilling life. Feel free to contact any of the authors in this book, or the other books in this series.

The proceeds of this book will go to feeding many of the rural Balinese families that are struggling through the current pandemic.

Other books in the series are…

The Way of the Leader : A Journey of Riches, Book Twenty Four
https://www.amazon.com/dp/1925919285

The Attitude of Gratitude : A Journey of Riches, Book Twenty Three
https://www.amazon.com/dp/1925919269

Facing your Fears : A Journey of Riches, Book Twenty Two
https://www.amazon.com/dp/1925919218

Returning to Love : A Journey of Riches, Book Twenty One
https://www.amazon.com/dp/B08C54M2RB

Develop Inner Strength : A Journey of Riches, Book Twenty
https://www.amazon.com/dp/1925919153

Building your Dreams : A Journey of Riches, Book Nineteen
https://www.amazon.com/dp/B081KZCN5R

Liberate your Struggles : A Journey of Riches, Book Eighteen
https://www.amazon.com/dp/1925919099

In Search of Happiness : A Journey of Riches, Book Seventeen
https://www.amazon.com/dp/B07R8HMP3K

Tapping into Courage : A Journey of Riches, Book Sixteen
https://www.amazon.com/dp/B07NDCY1KY

The Power Healing : A Journey of Riches, Book Fifteen
https://www.amazon.com/dp/B07LGRJQ2S

The Way of the Entrepreneur: A Journey Of Riches, Book Fourteen
https://www.amazon.com/dp/B07KNHYR8V

Discovering Love and Gratitude: A Journey Of Riches, Book Thirteen
https://www.amazon.com/dp/B07H23Q6D1

Transformational Change: A Journey Of Riches, Book Twelve
https://www.amazon.com/dp/B07FYHMQRS

Finding Inspiration: A Journey Of Riches, Book Eleven
https://www.amazon.com/dp/B07F1LS1ZW

Building your Life from Rock Bottom: A Journey Of Riches, Book Ten
https://www.amazon.com/dp/B07CZK155Z

Transformation Calling: A Journey Of Riches, Book Nine
https://www.amazon.com/dp/B07BWQY9FB

Letting Go and Embracing the New: A Journey Of Riches, Book Eight
https://www.amazon.com/dp/B079ZKT2C2

Making Empowering Choices: A Journey Of Riches, Book Seven
https://www.amazon.com/Making-Empowering-Choices-Journey-Riches-ebook/dp/B078JXMK5V

The Benefit of Challenge: A Journey Of Riches, Book Six
https://www.amazon.com/dp/B0778S2VBD

Personal Changes: A Journey Of Riches, Book Five
https://www.amazon.com/dp/B075WCQM4N

Dealing with Changes in Life: A Journey Of Riches, Book Four
https://www.amazon.com/dp/B0716RDKK7

Making Changes: A Journey Of Riches, Book Three
https://www.amazon.com/dp/B01MYWNI5A

The Gift In Challenge: A Journey Of Riches, Book Two
https://www.amazon.com/dp/B01GBEML4G

From Darkness into the Light: A Journey Of Riches, Book One
https://www.amazon.com/dp/B018QMPHJW

Thank you to all the authors who have shared aspects of their lives, hoping that it will inspire others to live a bigger version of themselves. I heard a great saying from Jim Rohn, "You can't complain and feel grateful at the same time." At any given moment, we have a choice to either feel like a victim of life, or be connected and grateful for it. I hope this book helps you to feel grateful and inspires you to go after your dreams. For more information about contributing to the series, visit http://ajourneyofriches.com/. Furthermore, if you enjoyed reading this book, we would appreciate your review on Amazon to help get our message out to more readers.

Made in the USA
Las Vegas, NV
07 June 2021

24323888R00133